THE LED GROW BOOK

Third Edition Preview

CHRISTOPHER H. SLOPER

Edited by Laurie Lamberth
Images by Laurie Lamberth

ISBN-13: 978-1-7045-2981-3

Forward

This is a special edition of The LED Grow Book, brought you by FOHSE - the Future of Horticulture Science and Engineering. It's a <u>preview</u> of the third edition that is exclusively distributed by FOHSE. The final version of the third edition will be available from Amazon in early to mid-2020.

Got questions about FOHSE lighting technology or about anything you read in this book? We're glad to help. Contact us at 888.FOHSE.77 or on the web at fohse.com

Christopher Sloper
Chief Horticultural Officer
sloper@fohse.com

Acknowledgements

There are two people who are primarily responsible for inspiring the completion of this edition:

Many of the new topics in this version were aided by **Brian Gandy**. We've spent countless hours "nerding out" about all things plant related. He has seriously helped me increase my knowledge and hopefully I've taught him a thing or two.

Brett Stevens has changed the way I perceive my role within the industry. As good CEO's do, he has increased my confidence in my abilities exponentially. I'm very excited about the opportunity he has provided and consider it an honor to be part of team FOHSE. Let's go change the way the world thinks about cultivating cannabis!

And as always, thanks to my amazing editor **Laurie Lamberth**. I never would have started this adventure without her. I'm glad she picked up "that call".

Thanks guys!

Table of Contents

Introduction

Once again, I can't believe how much has changed since the last edition of this book was published. Looking back, when the first edition of The LED Grow Book was published in 2013, small "burple" grow lights such as the original LED UFO dominated the tiny LED grow light market. These lights, with low-power emitters and limited coverage areas, were mostly used in hobby and experimental grows. There were no commercial LED grow lights on the market. HID lights dominated, and a lot of people thought "LEDs will never grow cannabis".

By the time the second edition was published in 2017, a few commercial-grade LED grow lights were finding their way into the emerging legalized cannabis industry, mostly for trials. Most commercial head growers had recently "graduated" from illicit warehouse and basement grows. The HID vs. LED debate raged. LED chip manufacturers were rapidly innovating their products, and our understanding of how light spectra affected plant growth was advancing quite rapidly.

As we approach 2020, cannabis legalization is sweeping across the U.S. and around the globe, and with it has come massive investment in large-scale cannabis grow facilities. I, personally, have installed thousands of commercial-grade LED grow lights in large-scale grow facilities in many U.S. states, with a pipeline that includes grow facilities many other countries. Elite growers are finally embracing LED grow lights and reaping the rewards. LED grow experience will soon be a requirement for top-level cannabis cultivation jobs.

Several trends are driving the adoption of LED grow lights in these large-scale cannabis cultivation facilities. LED emitters have improved dramatically and the way they are being used within an LED grow light fixture is radically different than before. LED emitters are being mounted in large light fixtures that emit a flat plane of light, which illuminates a large area of plant canopy with amazing intensity and uniformity. Our understanding of how plants consume and convert light into growth has advanced such that full-spectrum white light now dominates, often supplemented by additional light spectra (red, far-red, UV). Point-source grow lights such as HIDs and burple grow lights are on their way out.

Legalization is also lifting the stigma associated with cannabis cultivation, and so professionals from other industries are finding their way into the grow room and bringing their technology skills with them. From automation to process control to wireless communication, these skills are transforming how commercial grow operations are run and improving the quality and quantity of harvests. The Internet of Things (IoT) has found a strong foothold in the grow room.

With these innovations comes one significant downside: the experienced growers who created and maintained the illicit cannabis industry for decades find themselves shut out of the new cannabis game. Prior run-ins with the law have benched many: the new corporate cannabis industry requires clean criminal records. Old-school cannabis growers also don't want to be told what they can and can't do: in particular, they don't want someone telling them what they can and can't spray on their plants as a part of an integrated pest management program. Because of this, I routinely work with "head growers" who have one to three years of experience and are running large, multi-million dollar grow facilities. Many of them don't have a clue about what they are doing, and they often make simple mistakes that create large impacts. This will change over time as the commercial cannabis industry grows up.

The inrush of money and talent is unfortunately also bringing out a lot of "me too" players. There are many new LED grow light manufacturers looking to cash in. The hobby side of the market has exploded, with hundreds or thousands of manufacturers trying to make a buck. Dozens of new manufacturers have entered the commercial LED grow light market, but only a few of them are bringing cutting-edge technology. Now more than ever is the time to do your homework when selecting an LED grow light. One of the goals of this book is to educate you, so that selecting the proper LED grow lighting system can be easy.

Why Update This Book?

That's easy – there's lots to update! The cannabis industry has gotten more sophisticated in the last few years. Topics that I felt were a distraction are now relevant. The lexicon of the industry is maturing. We're ready for more thoughtful conversations about cultivation and I'm doing my part to advance these discussions even further.

I've added a bunch of new content including my thoughts on vapor pressure deficit (VPD), added a detailed explanation of how RuBisCO works, and introduced a new topic which is blue light toxicity. There many updates to my original thinking, such as new thoughts on UV light and the Emerson Enhancement Effect.

Something else is new: until recently commercial LED grow light manufacturer were developing flowering lights as direct replacements to the traditional 1000 watt high pressure sodium (HPS) lamp. This strategy was based on how much one could save on electrical costs by deploying LED technology. This an old way of thinking.

What matters more is high photosynthetic photon flux densities (PPFD). Don't worry if you don't know that term as you will by the end of the book. For now let's just say it's a fancy way of saying high light levels. This represents a shift in thinking from "how much can I save" to "how much can I produce". Much of the new content of this book focuses on how to grow huge harvests under high light levels utilizing this concept.

Who Should Read This Book?

Everyone who is even considering <u>any</u> type of indoor garden–lit by LEDs or otherwise–should read this book. I've added tons of tips gained from personal experience that will make any gardener more successful. Both hobby and commercial growers will find a great deal of useful information even if you read the last editions–there's that much new content.

I have gotten a great deal of feedback on the first two editions though online reviews and conversations with friends and peers. Some said it was too technical, others disagreed and thought it needed much more geeky content. It sounds like I hit that balance just about right!

I've decided to take the advice of both sides and make this edition more technical while also simplifying it as much as possible. I'll let you know when a section or chapter is aimed at the hobby crowd or more suited for the commercial guys. Unless otherwise described, this book is for everyone who wants to successfully garden indoors.

How This Book Is Organized

We'll start the discussion off with a review of correct plant light terminology and discuss why many common lighting terms are wrong for gardening purposes. Next the conversation heads to why we would want to use an LED grow light in the first place. Following that we will chat a bit about what we are trying to accomplish with indoor garden lighting, which is to drive photosynthesis and photomorphogenesis. Next we focus on the tool we've selected–the LED grow light. And finally we'll discuss how to grow with LEDs.

As you read this book, you'll come across tips for better gardening, enclosed in boxes by category:

 Sloper Says

Insights gained from my personal gardening experience.

 SAFETY FIRST

Things that could be dangerous to plants or people.

 Zen Gardening

Making gardening easier and more peaceful.

 Fun Fact

Funny or unexpected information about gardening.

 Good Practice

Gardening practices that help you grow heavy, high-quality harvests.

 EXPERT CORNER

In-depth material for those who'd like to learn more.

1: Lighting Defined

Before we can get started, there are many terms that need to be explained so we are on the same wavelength… yes that was a bad pun! If we don't use the same terms the same way we will never communicate successfully.

I have spent lots of time at trade shows helping clients promote their LED grow lights and have noticed a trend. The location of the booth, in relationship to the entrance, determined the questions I received. That is, which LED grow light manufacturer an attendee talked to first dictated the questions they asked.

These experiences have taught me that many LED grow light manufacturers don't know, or at least don't use, correct lighting terminology. They mix up or misuse much of the technical information about their lights, making it difficult for end users and buyers to understand the manufacturer's lights and how they compare to others. How about we clean some of this confusion up?

While the material in this chapter may seem super-geeky at first glance, think of it as a reference to be used while reading the rest of the book. Give it a quick skim and move on to the next chapter if it's too much info to digest at once.

Units Matter

Maybe it's the chemist in me showing through, but one point I must drive home is that reporting a number without its units is utterly useless. Far too often I see LED grow light manufacturers leaving off units of measure when describing their lights, or even worse using the wrong ones. Ask yourself, if someone advertises that their LED grow light has a performance level of "3.0" does that mean anything to you? Now 3.0 $\mu mol/J$ has meaning… at least to some of us. By the time you're done reading this chapter it will for you too.

Understanding how things interact can often be cleared up by carefully examining the underlying units. They can tell their own story and guide you. When you're working out the lighting design for your grow, be sure to take the time to understand and use the correct lighting terms and units. Mistakes can be discovered much more quickly when you paint a complete picture of what's going on in your grow that is informed by correct terminology and measurements as well as observations and experience. Using the correct units is not just for LED grow lights. Regardless of the lighting source, units need to be used universally and need to be correct.

Qualitative vs. Quantitative

There are two types of measurements we collect: qualitative and quantitative. Qualitative information does not contain numeric values. It's a description rather than a result. In contrast, quantitative data does contain numbers. For example, a qualitative observation would be that a solution turned blue, while a quantitative result would be that the solution turned 460nm blue.

Efficiency vs. Efficacy

Do you know the difference between efficiency and efficacy? Although some may think I'm nitpicking there is an actual, technical difference between the two. I discovered recently that I have been using these terms incorrectly for just about my whole life.

The basic distinction is that efficiency is "unit less". It's a ratio of one thing to another, with both measurements represented by the same unit and reported as a percentage. For the non-math types, the units cancel themselves out. Think of a car's drivetrain—if the engine produces 100 horsepower and 90 horsepower is measured at the wheels the transmission is .90 or 90% efficient.

On the other hand, efficacy does have units. Efficacy is the term used when two things are compared and the units don't match (don't cancel each other out). Continuing with our car example, how far a car can travel on a gallon of gas is referred to as miles per gallon (miles / gallon). A vehicle that gets 20 miles / gallon has greater efficacy than one that get 10 miles / gallon.

Measuring Light

There are two important tools for measuring light for plant growth. These are an integrating sphere for the manufacturer and a quantum meter/sensor for growers.

Integrating Sphere

An integrating sphere's job is to "count" the number of individual photons emitted by a lamp or fixture. As the name implies, it's a spherical device that light a source being tested is placed inside. Once the light source comes up to operating temperature (typically about 30 minutes), total photon output is tested and reported as photosynthetic photon flux (PPF) for gardening applications. This is the most accurate way to measure PPF.

Integrating spheres can be used for other applications such as reflectance or transmittance testing of materials. Various internal coatings (typically barium sulfate or PTFE) and the types of light detectors used determine the sphere's function, thus, integrating spheres are designed specifically for a given task. As you can imagine, integrating spheres can be very, very expensive especially large ones.

While it's not practical or necessary for an end user to have one, any serious LED grow light manufacturer or research and development facility will have an integrating sphere. These facilities do not solely rely on third party testing or manufacturers' specification sheets to develop, test or research lighting products. Development and testing cycles can also be shortened by cutting out turnaround times for outside testing. An LED grow light manufacturer's investment in an integrating sphere signals a strong commitment to the industry and means they will be more likely to still be in business down the road if warranty work is needed.

Even LED grow light manufacturers with their own integrating spheres still need outside validation to verify their specifications. Do not invest in a commercial grade LED grow light that does not have third-party photometrics available. There are way too many manufacturers claiming "out of this world" performance metrics for their LED grow lights–I say make them prove them! Certification bodies such as Underwriters Lab (UL) have testing programs for grow lights. They take performance measurements and publicly post the results. I strongly suggest you look up a potential light and verify its performance via a third-party source.

Note that most hobby LED grow companies don't have an integrating sphere. They might not even know what one is and that's ok. They are not developing lights that commercial operations will rely upon, that is, nobody's paycheck is on the line with a closet grow.

Lastly, size matters: Integrating spheres can vary in size from very small (a few centimeters in diameter) up to fairly large (up to 3 meters in diameter). A typical integrating sphere used to test LED grow lights is 2 meters in diameter, a large size that comes with a large price tag.

Quantum Meter

Quantum meters directly measure the number of photons hitting the surface of the sensor and are how we measure photosynthetic photon flux density (PPFD). Quantum meters must be specifically tuned for the lighting source being measured. A meter calibrated for HID lighting sources may not give accurate measurements for LEDs and vice versa.

Note that some older quantum sensors have an upper cut off point at ~655nm. Since red 660nm emitters are included in many LED grow lights, you're not measuring the full output of those chips with an old sensor. This will make your readings lower than what is actually being delivered. The actual loss cannot be easily converted as it depends on the photon output above 655nm. The more 660nm chips in the fixture, the more the PPFD measurements taken with an older sensor will be off.

Of the many quantum meters currently on the market, two are suitable for accurately measuring LED PPFD: LI-COR model LI-190R with LI-250A Light Meter or the Apogee Instruments model MQ-500 Full Spectrum Quantum Meter. Other, lesser quality quantum meters may grossly underestimate the PPFD measurement for LED products.

Be sure to take measurements at the top of the plants in the same manner as the garden is operated. For example, if you are a hobby grower in a closet, take your readings with the door closed or as closed as possible. For commercial grows with numerous grow lights, make sure to keep the sensor away from your body. You can inadvertently block light from an adjacent fixture if you're not careful.

Plant Lighting Terms

Photosynthetically Active Radiation (PAR) is the *qualitative* description of the radiation between 400nm and 700nm and is similar to visible light spectrum for humans. There is no weighting factor for PAR (unlike for human visual metrics), and the number of photons of light in this range is the widely accepted measurement for light that supports plant growth. There are no units for PAR.

Photosynthetic Photon Flux (PPF) is the *quantitative* measurement of how many PAR photons a fixture produces. The units for this measurement are micromoles per second (μmol/s). This metric is obtained by using an integrating sphere or a flat-plane integration measurement. Though this metric indicates how much PAR a fixture is producing, it doesn't indicate where that light is going.

Photosynthetic Photon Flux Density (PPFD) is the *quantitative* measurement of how much of the PPF is delivered to a particular target (or canopy surface area). The units for this measurement are micromoles per square meter second ($\mu mol\ m^{-2}\ s^{-1}$) or sometimes written $\mu mol/m^2$ s. This metric is obtained using a quantum sensor and meter.

Maybe I am being super nerdy, but $\mu mol/m^2/s$ is technically incorrect. It's the second "/" that cause the problem. Since the units are not bound to each other (such as velocity that is measured in m/s), these units would be rearranged. Mathematically $\mu mol/m^2/s$ rearranges to $\mu mol\ s/m^2$ which is definitely wrong.

Photon Flux Density (PFD) is the measurement of how many photons a fixture produces regardless whether they fall into the PAR range. This measurement includes both the UV and far-red ranges. Like PPFD, the units for this measurement are micromoles per square meter second ($\mu mol\ m^{-2}\ s^{-1}$).

Yield Photon Flux (YPF) weights photons in the range from 380 to 760nm based on plant's photosynthetic response measured micromoles per second (μmol/s). Whereas all PPF photons are born equal, YPF considers the relative photosynthetic efficiency of different wavelengths of light, assigning less weight to less useful light. The problem with YPF is it was developed based on short-term measurements that were made on single leaves in low light, rather than whole plants under light levels similar to those used in commercial grow facilities.

Plant Biologically Active Radiation Flux (PBAR Flux) is the amount of energy measured from 350-800nm and is also expressed in units of micromoles per second (μmol/s). It represents the total theorized portion of the electromagnetic spectrum that influences plant processes.

Watt (W) is a derived unit of power. The unit is defined as 1 joule per second (J/s) and can be used to express the rate of energy conversion or transfer with respect to time. From a thermal load, one watt is equal to 3.41 British Thermal Units per hour (BTU/h).

Photoperiod is the total amount of time the lights are turned on during a single day. Short-day crops like cannabis have a 12-hour photoperiod when flowering, and a longer photoperiod of up to 18 hours during the vegetative growth phase.

PAR Photon Efficacy (PPE) is the measurement of how a fixture converts power (watts) into PAR photons. Since power is a rate of energy, the appropriate unit to describe this is joules per second (J/s). Dividing the PPF by the actual watts used to create it (measured at the plug), results in units of micromole per Joule (μmol/J).

Photon Efficacy (PE) is a newer term that has been introduced recently into the controlled-environment agriculture (CEA) market. It's another way to describe photon efficacy but includes photons that fall outside the PAR range such as the UV and far-red regions.

Target Efficiency (or Coefficient of Utilization) is the amount of light that actually hits the target canopy area and measured as a percentage (%). Directional sources like LEDs can be upwards of 85% target efficient while typical HIDs are 65% or lower.

Daily Light Integral (DLI) is a measurement of how many PAR photons a plant receives in a day. DLI is the most important number when it comes to plant growth it describes the daily dose of PAR photons. DLI is measured in units of moles per square meter day (mol m^{-2} day^{-1}) and is the result of PPFD x photoperiod.

High Intensity Discharge (HID) is a collective term for high pressure sodium (HPS), metal halide (MH) and ceramic metal halide (CMH) lamps. For the purpose of this book they can be considered interchangeable. They all create light from super-heated plasma and are non-directional.

A **Photon** is a single packet of light energy at a specific wavelength measured in nanometers (nm). Photon/photons are sometimes called quantum/quanta.

Spectral Power Distribution (SPD) is a chart that shows the radiant power emitted at each wavelength from 360 to 770nm by a light source. A spectrophotometer is used to collect the data. You are probably already familiar with SPD charts as they are printed on the packaging of just about every HID lamp to show its spectral output.

The **Inverse Square Law** is states that for every unit of distance away from a light source the light intensity is decreased by the square of the distance. The law is based on a point source of light. The application of this law is rooted in understanding light height and the effect of moving it up or down.

Since LED grow lights use many individual emitters mounted on a flat plane (not a point of light like a HID lamp) the concept of a **"Modified" Inverse Square Law** should be considered. Basically what this means is the intensity a LED grow light will be greater than predicted by the inverse square law due to the fixture having so many sources of light.

Stark-Einstein Law states that for every quantum (photon) that is absorbed, one electron will be excited, regardless of the photon's energy, between 400nm and 700nm. This law is the fundamental basis of why more light equals more harvestable weight and why the wavelength of the photon does not matter when driving photosynthesis.

Haitz's Law states that "every decade, the cost per lumen falls by a factor of 10, the amount of light generated per LED package increases by a factor of 20, for a given wavelength of light". So far in the real world, this law is holding true.

Uniformity describes how evenly a fixture distributes light over a surface area is calculated by light mapping software. Minimum/average illumination is the most common method used to measure uniformity on a light map. The scale of these measurements extends from 0 to 1 with 1.0 being perfect uniformity. A result of 0.85 means 85% uniformity.

Human Lighting Terms

As you can tell, the science of measuring light gets complicated fast. Most of us are used to describing lighting in terms of human perception not plants. None of the terms below are useful in describing plant lighting. I've included them as reference so you understand why they are useless for plant lighting conversations. If you hear someone using the following terms relating to plants, correct them!

Luminous Flux, better known by its scientific unit–the **lumen** (lm), is a measure of the total quantity of visible light emitted by a source in all directions. It's based on how much light is perceived by <u>humans</u> at the peak of the daylight (photopic) vision curve and is focused heavily on the green portion of the visible light spectrum.

Lux is simply lumens per square meter. Since lumens are for <u>humans</u> who cares how many of them there are per area.

Foot Candles is an illumination unit that expresses "the illuminance cast on a surface by a one-candela source one foot away." One foot-candle is equal to one lumen per square foot or approximately 10.764 lux. Again, since lumens are for <u>humans</u> who cares.

Color Rendering Index (CRI) describes how a light source makes the color of an object appear to <u>human</u> eyes. CRI describes how a light source compares to a reference, as a percentage. The standard reference is a 2700 Kelvin incandescent light source weighted at 100%.

Color Corrected Temperature (CCT) is used in cinematography, photography, stage lighting, and television. CCT is the process of altering the visual appearance (think cool vs. warm) of white light in a scene. Filters are used on the camera or the light source is altered to create the desired Kelvin temperature.

Lumen Depreciation Terms

LED lighting is different to other sources as they don't burn out–they just gradually decline in light production. Lumen depreciation describes how the output of a light source declines over its useful life. Even though these ratings are about lumens, they can give us a good indication of overall photon decay of LED grow lights over time. Lumen and photon decay can be similar assuming the light does not contain a significant amount of green light.

The following terms were created by the Illuminating Engineering Society of North America (IESNA) to describe lumen depreciation in LED sources:

L90, L80, and L70 describe when 90%, 80% and 70% respectively of the initial lumens emitted by an LED are depreciated to the respective levels of output. These tests are conducted at three different temperatures and each level is calculated for each temperature. For humans, lumen loss is not very noticeable until L70 or 70% reduction in light output.

LM-80 reports the luminous flux for a given current over a 6,000-hour period with interval measurements, at three different temperatures: 55°C, 85°C and a third temperature selected by the manufacturer. LM-80 tests individual lighting components such as an individual LED package or array—not a complete fixture.

TM-21 takes the data from the LM-80 test and makes a prediction of the useful life of the complete fixture of lamp source. It is a calculation rather than a direct measurement.

LM-79 is a measurement of the LED light as a complete lighting system reporting on:

- Total luminous flux
- Luminous intensity distribution
- Electrical power characteristics
- Luminous efficacy (calculated)
- Color characteristics (CRI, CCT)

L90 vs. L70

For LED grow lights, you need to focus on "L90" data when considering the longevity of a fixture. LED emitters degrade over time: L90 predicts when light output will drop to 90% of the initial output. When a fixture output drops below L90 it's time to replace it. The good news is that a properly designed LED grow light with high-quality emitters can reach L90 at 50,000+ hours. Unfortunately there are LED grow light manufacturers who are using L70 data for making claims about a product's useful life. Be warned, do your homework and demand L90 data.

Other Incorrect Lighting Measurements

There are a whole bunch of other incorrect lighting measurements that are commonly tossed around when someone is attempting to describe plant lighting. All of the terms below should <u>never</u> be used when discussing plant lighting.

Irradiance (W/m^2) was the standard measurement of light output when I started in this industry decades ago. Until recently, the indoor gardening community recommended 50 watts of lighting per square foot as a starting point.

The problem is you have no idea of how much PPFD this translates into. Meters were very expensive back then especially the correct one—a quantum meter. With quantum meter pricing coming down from the stratosphere, the gardening industry has been able to move on from this blunt estimate. Irradiance can be useful when calculating electrical circuit loads and heat output. It's still commonly used by greenhouse growers today.

Plants per Area is a terrible measurement but I hear it all the time. What's important is canopy surface area not how many stems support it. Some growers my elect to have lots of small plants with small canopies and short veg times while others may choose to have larger plants with large canopies and longer veg times. Each grower has to calculate the economics of these decisions and find what works for them. Instead growers should develop a new mind set – it's not about the plants, it's about the total canopy. Consider yourself to be in the canopy business not the plant business!

Commercial Grade LED Grow Lights Defined

There is quite a big difference between an LED grow light designed for hobby use and a one designed for a commercial grow operation. Don't get me wrong–there is nothing wrong with many of the hobby grade lights available on the market. You just don't want to use them in a commercial operation because they are missing many of the characteristics required for safe and effective commercial use, including:

- High PPF output (µmol/s)
- High PAR photon efficacy (µmol/J)
- PPFD levels suitable for the crop
- High target efficiency
- Wet location rated (or better)
- A broad spectrum for both plants and the grower
- Matches or surpasses HID production/yield/quality
- LED emitters physically protected from environment
- Durable construction that can be banged into without damage
- An optimized spectrum for maximizing photosynthesis and photomorphogenesis

Burple

A serious problem with many LED grow lights is their "burple" color. Burple is a loosely-coined industry term to describe the purple-ish light emitted by lights with only blue and red LEDs. There are several problems with burple.

First, these lights can seriously reduce visual acuity while working under them. Our eyes are focused more on green/yellow, the center of the visible spectrum, which is exactly the opposite of burple. Even small exposures to burple light will cause havoc to your eyes when returning to normal light. This problem is so pronounced that there are manufacturers producing protective eyeglasses that make it easier to work under burple LED grow lights. If you have never had the fun of working under burple you're not missing anything. Even with corrective glasses you just feel a bit sick to your stomach. The effect is so pronounced it can even mess with your vision in a greenhouse during the day.

The second problem with burple is that it hides many gardening problems because they can't be seen easily. Common problems such as pests and molds can go completely unnoticed. Plant nutritional deficiencies, that could easily be corrected and save the garden, will hide too since the plants look purple or even black under burple.

Blue Light Toxicity

There is a serious health issue with burple grow lights that is not being discussed nearly enough – burple is really bad for humans. Our eyes use red, green and blue cones to perceive colors with a maximum daytime sensitivity at 555nm (green). When there is no green in what we are seeing, our eyes attempt to adjust up to a point of nearly full dilation. Unfortunately this allows full blue light exposure to the retina.

According to a study at the University of Toledo, when retinol (a molecule within our eyes that allows people to see) is exposed to blue light it kills photoreceptor cells within the eye. It's a very serious condition because these cells cannot be regenerated.

Several years ago I had a client who operated a large microgreen facility lit up with burple LEDs. On my second visit I wore my color correcting glasses and the head grower chuckled at me for wearing them. He mentioned that for the first few years he worked there his eyes were "messed up" when going into sunlight after working in the grow. He said that over the time he "got used to the color shift" and it didn't affect him any more. In his mind, he adapted to the burple working environment. I told him that his experience was likely due to damage to his eyes, and to see an eye doctor right away to see if anything could be done. Unfortunately it was probably too late.

Personally, I don't understand why OSHA (or the equivalent in your country) has not shut down the use of burple LED grow lights in commercial grow facilities.

2: Why LED Grow Lights?

There are many good reasons to consider using LED grow lights. These include lower operating costs (especially in states such as California with insanely expensive electrical rates), less associated labor expenses (no need to relamp), easy to clean (with the right light), improved uniformity, increased terpenes, a potential reduction in hazardous waste and the ability to deliver custom light spectra to the garden.

Cheaper to Operate/Return on Investment

Are LED grow lights expensive? I guess that all depends on how you look at it. Regardless of your current opinion, I bet by the time you're done with this section you'll understand the economic advantage of LED grow lights.

In 2013, when I published the first edition of this book, LED grow lights were four to five times the cost of a high quality HID lighting setup. LEDs were still in their infancy: you might have seen a stop light or two being converted to LEDs but that was about it. Flash forward to 2019 when I wrote this edition and LED grow lights were a bit less than three times as expensive as a typical HID grow light. Some hobby lights were less than twice the price of HID at this point in time. These comparative price levels are the first major step LED grow light have taken toward reducing the time it takes for LED grow light return on investment (ROI) to go positive.

Lighting Cost Reduction

Most of the cost recovery from LED grow lights comes from electrical service savings. Because of their greater photon efficiency compared to HIDs, commercial grade LED grow lights typically use about 40% less electricity to produce the same number of photons as their HID counterparts. You would be hard pressed to find another way to slash 40% out of the largest expense in any business with a single change.

Properly designed LED grow lights have a long useful life with some rated to over 10 years. I personally don't believe anyone will use a given light longer than 5 years. The technology is rapidly changing and there will be better lights within a realistic business investment horizon of 5-6 years.

Re-Lamp Cost Reduction

Depending on their re-lamping strategy, HID gardeners will replace their lamps 4-9 times during a 5-year time period. This comes at a cost of $50-150 per lamp not including labor and potential downtime losses. This cost saving alone can make up a big chunk of the difference in the cost of LED grow lights. LEDs are starting to not look so expensive in comparison, huh?

Keep in mind labor is never free. For the hobby growers with only a lamp or two to change this might not be a big deal. For a commercial facility with hundreds of lights per room and dozens of rooms, this can be a daunting and expensive task. I don't know why but most people ignore labor expense in ROI calculations.

Cooling Cost Reduction

The third major saving with LED gardens is reduced cooling costs. Traditionally, cooling consumes a large part of total energy used in an indoor garden. Since LED grow lights emit less heat, there Is less to remove, leading to savings in both utility bills and air cooling equipment.

I know what I'm going to say next may offend some HVAC professionals but a general rule of thumb we use in the lighting industry is that for every three watts of lighting reduced, air conditioning is reduced by one watt. If we assume a ~40% reduction in lighting watts compared to HID, this works out to a potential 13% reduction in electricity consumed by your HVAC system when switching to LED grow lights. Your actual results may vary!

Environment, grow room configuration, crop selection, air flow, and many other factors influence HVAC needs and related HVAC energy consumption. That said, using less watts for grow lighting will cause less lighting watts to decay into the growing environment as heat. Less HVAC is likely needed, though you should consult an HVAC specialist with a strong record is supporting successful grow facilities to determine your actual savings.

Vertical Farming

Many commercial grows are in warehouses with tall ceilings. Why not take advantage of the height and add one or more levels? Every level you add cuts down the cost per square foot of growing space you're paying in rent. You're paying for the whole space anyway why not double or better your output for the same rent expense?

Vertical farming designs can be very simple such as the solid, stationary racking found at your local big-box hardware store. More sophisticated vertical farm designs include motorized, movable racking systems that roll across the floor sideways similar to moveable library shelves. Although movable growing systems have higher upfront cost, they need only one aisle width of non-production space for the entire grow room again increasing the grow footprint of the facility.

LEDs are the perfect lights for vertical farming due to their low profile and passive cooling. LED grow light manufacturers have begun to design light panels specifically for vertical farming. This is another area to keep an eye on as the technology continues to develop.

CFOs LOVE vertical farming: potentially doubling (or tripling+) the potential harvest out of the same square footage is financially alluring. Those who have actually worked in large vertical farms typically can't say the same. Before you jump in, there are considerations to examine.

Water Leaks: First off, when vertical farming, make sure EVERYTHING is watertight. It's only a matter of when (and how bad) you have spills in a traditional, single-level grow. Growing vertically doubles (or more) the opportunities for spills. Make sure all the components (not just the lights) in the vertical racks are waterproof with minimum of an IP55 rating.

Additionally, make sure your power cords are plugged into watertight connections/sockets. Nutrient solutions will find their way into any open electrical connection and let you know that leaks exist!

Labor Stress A second major consideration for vertical farming is its effect on your grow room staff. It is far easier for them to work with plants on a single level than to climb up and down on a ladder or ride a lift. All the extra bending, stretching and lifting will wear them out. I can always tell when it's harvest day when I visit vertical farm as the employees are spent. If they get too burned out, you'll run the risk of them making mistakes or even quitting. I've seen it happen many times.

Powered Lifts A powered lift can help reduce some of the physical labor of the employees in a vertical grow. That said, they have a downside. Since the lift comes in contact with the plants, how do you sanitize it? Can you effectively reach all the nooks and crannies in a powered lift with a cleaning agent? To limit exposure, each room should have its own dedicated equipment including the lift.

Powered lifts can limit the number of people working in a particular room as they fill an entire aisle width. Without a powered lift, you can split the aisle width between two rows allowing more people access more areas of the garden at the same time. Another consideration is that powered lifts are not cheap. Having one (or more) per room can get expensive quickly.

Veg'ing in Vertical Farms

Vertical farming can be manageable for plants in the vegetative state. With lower light demands and shorter plants, the tiers can be spaced fairly close together allowing access by a step stool or a smaller ladder.

With lower light levels, heat also tends to be less of an issue since fewer photons are generated and less heat as well. One issue to consider is air movement within the potentially tight tiers of vertical veg farms. As the tiers become more dense, wall fans cannot effectively circulate the room air. Installing fans within the tiers can add a bunch of complexity. Again, if you are going to install fans within the tiers make sure they are at least IP55 rated.

Flowering in Vertical Farms

In small farms (a few hundred square feet of canopy per room), vertical flowering can be manageable. Air flow can be managed without too much fuss. One person can manage it so the aisles do not become crowded. As grow facilities get larger and larger (multi thousands of square feet of canopy per room), even two flowering tiers can become challenging. Going beyond two levels on a large scale adds a significant level of complexity on every dimension including air flow, irrigation, labor, heat management and pest management.

How are you actually going to remove excess heat from a 3+ tier configuration? Where are you going to place HVAC registers and returns so the room has a consistent temperature? Heat management in a single level can be problematic. It's only more difficult with more levels.

Another potential problem is how rising heat affects the root zone in the upper tiers. With the upper tiers being naturally hotter, are those root zones cool enough? Root zones that are too warm (74+°F/23+°C and above) are the perfect breeding ground for everything that wants to attack your grow. From molds to legged beasts, pests will love the warmth if given a chance.

Sloper Says

Grow media + nutrients + warm temperatures = petri dish wailing to grow something! Manage your root zone temperatures.

Calculating Return on Investment

It's really not that hard to do your own return on investment calculations. Anyone with some Excel skills can work up a spreadsheet and figure your own payback period. Simply divide the upfront cost of buying an LED grow light by the cost savings expected per year. That will give you the number of years it will take to "pay back" your investment in the light–that is your ROI. If computers are not your thing, work it out with a pencil and paper. If that's still not you bag, just about any decent LED grow light manufacturer can help you with these calculations.

I've conducted many ROI studies for my clients. In my experience, even with cheap electrical rates, payback periods for new LED grow light installs can be under two years and under three for retrofitting from HID technology. Where electricity is expensive the payback period can be even quicker.

Reduced Fire Threat

The superheating of gasses in HID lamps presents a real-world fire threat. In the fall of 2018, there were two fires in the Las Vegas area caused by HID lamps exploding. In both cases extremely hot shards of glass landed on plastic grow tables which caused them to catch fire. Although neither facility suffered physical damage there was total crop loss due to smoke.

Who would want to consume anything that was exposed to plastic smoke? In both cases the cost of retrofitting with LEDs was less than the crop loss. If these facilities had converted to LEDs and not started the fires, the lights would have paid for themselves.

Increasing Electrical Rates

When have electrical rates ever gone down? Electrical demand increases every day, and in order to keep up, electric companies are continuously deploying new infrastructure and passing along the costs to customers. Increasing electrical rates provide significant incentives to switch to LED grow lights now. A 1000 watt high-intensity discharge (HID) light running a 12-hour bloom cycle every day uses 4.3 megawatts of electricity in a year. Even with cheap electricity at $0.12 per kilowatt-hour, it costs more than $500 per year to run one 1000 watt grow light, and that does not include the electricity to maintain the environment. LED grow lights can cut that expenditure in half or more.

Increased Terpenes

Another reason for loving LED grow lights is the quality of the harvest they produce. In my opinion, LED-grown crops are *significantly* better than crops grown with any other light source I have tried. I attribute this mostly to increased terpene production typically seen when growing the same plants under LED grow lights vs. HIDs.

 **Fun Fact**

The class of compounds called terpenes are actually named after turpentine. Every once in a while, science names something easy!

Terpenes are a large and diverse class of organic chemicals responsible for smells and flavors. While conifers (think pine trees) are one of the largest producers, a wide variety of plants and even a few insects produce terpenes. Terpenes are aromatic, with turpentine being the most familiar. The relationship between garden lights and terpene production is yet another area that needs significant research.

Reduction in Hazardous Waste

Another reason to switch to LED grow lights is that they generate less waste. As mentioned previously, commercial HID gardeners replace their lamps as often as every six months, hobbyists generally once a year, creating quite a bit of waste. Some of these spent lamps contain mercury and must be disposed of as toxic waste, but unfortunately many of them end up in the trash—adding heavy metals to our landfills that can leach into the water supply. This toxic waste stream is completely eliminated with LED grow lights, though the grow lights themselves must be disposed of as "e-waste" (similar to computers) at the end or their useful lives.

While some HID lamp manufacturers have removed the mercury from their bulbs, many of the cheap lamps still contain it. Besides the disposal issue, these lamps may also generate a bigger toxic waste problem: heavy metals on your crop. Some lighting research shows that mercury-containing lamps can "spray" vaporized mercury onto the garden. While not all lighting experts agree with this controversial finding, why take the chance that your grow light could poison your crop?

Other Savings for the Hobby Grower

This next section is primarily for hobby growers, though you commercial guys should give it a quick read for fresh ideas.

Further Cooling Cost Reductions

Air conditioners may no longer be needed for small gardens: you may be able to control garden temperatures using exhaust fans to vent heated air out of the garden and intake fans draw cooler outside air in. Not running A/C can save a lot of energy, plus it eliminates the chance of ozone-depleting gasses escaping from a damaged or leaky unit.

You may be able to use smaller-capacity ventilation fans since there is less heat. If you use a single exhaust fan, don't go too small, as this fan has two jobs: to exchange the air in your garden and remove excess heat. Secondary exhaust fans used in the garden may be smaller or eliminated entirely, such as inline fans to vent air-cooled hoods. Smaller fans need smaller filters, another cost saver.

High-Temp Shut Down Controller

One of the most important safety devices in a HID garden—a high-temp shutdown system—drops from must-have to optional with LED grow lights. Since there is less heat produced with LED grow lights, the threat of a heat-based garden disaster is reduced if not eliminated altogether.

Fire Suppression

As above, the amount of heat generated by HID lamps and ballasts creates a real potential for a fire in your garden should something go seriously wrong. While any of the new cost effective, automatic fire-suppression products should be considered mandatory in any garden that uses 1000 watt HID lamps and are recommended for gardens lit by a single 400 or 600 watt HID, these systems are simply not required with LED grow lights. It's a good idea to always keep a fire extinguisher nearby "just in case".

Wall Coverings

Most indoor gardeners cover grow room walls with reflective material to bounce the unused light back into the garden. Since LEDs have a greater target efficiency than HIDs, it doesn't make sense to spend lots of money on expensive reflective wall coverings. Flat white paint is a lot cheaper and almost as good.

Be sure to use flat paint, since glossy paint is actually less reflective. White paint also makes it easy to see nutrient splashes or mold infestations that need to be cleaned up at the end of a grow run, and you don't have to clean as rigorously. When the grow space starts looking bad, repaint.

Space Requirements

While it doesn't generate direct cost savings, LED grow lights allow for plants to be grown in smaller spaces. With physically smaller lights, smaller fans, and less equipment in the grow room, people who previously could not find a suitable location in their home may discover that they can now grow indoors. You no longer need a full-height closet: half of one can be converted into a single-light grow space.

What's Wrong with HID Grow Lights?

All HID grow lights are effective at growing plants indoors when properly used. While each type has its pluses and minuses, HIDs have dominated the indoor garden market for decades despite their limitations—heat being the primary enemy.

HIDs do produce lots of photons that easily power photosynthesis. Using HPS and MH lamps in combination or switching between MH and HPS for vegetative and flowering stages, has worked for indoor gardeners for a long time. Why change?

The Most Un-Green Thing in Our Gardens

The first blow against HIDs is that they produce too much heat for the amount of light they generate. A 1000 watt HPS lamp is only about 40% efficient when it comes to growing plants: it produces approximately 400 watts of PAR plus 600 watts of "heat" energy above 700nm. The heat (and light) comes from superheating a mixture of mineral salts until they glow.

This waste heat must go somewhere. Unless removed, it will go straight into your garden's canopy–raising temperatures, speeding up transpiration, and eventually drying out both the plants and their growing media. Waste heat is expensive to produce and even more expensive to get rid of. Both sides of that equation needlessly burn electricity.

Wasted vs. Targeted Spectrum

Equally troublesome, most HIDs were designed to help humans see, not so that plants could grow under them. Their light spectrum is not optimal for photosynthesis: much of the light they emit is in the middle of the visible spectrum, where human eyesight is optimized but photosynthesis is not. HID lamp manufacturers have been able to tweak their lamp chemistries a little bit to create HID lamps with a more desirable spectrum for plants, such as the "blue enhanced" HPS lamps sold by indoor gardening centers. Still these lamps produce more heat than usable light.

HID lamp manufacturers can only go so far to improve their lamps without making major changes from the ground up, at great expense and with limited gain in performance. Not only are the possible improvements in HID lamp suitability for photosynthesis limited by technology, the indoor gardening market is tiny compared to the general lighting market. Research and development budgets for HID grow lights are small compared to those for street, parking lot, and stadium lights, so radical innovation is unlikely to emerge.

What's Holding LED Grow Lights Back?

Even with their advantages, several factors have been holding LED grow lights back. While the primary reason for slow adoption has been high upfront cost (by now you understand the economics of why this objection is wrong) additional factors still restrain large scale adoption. These include grower ego, LED emitter just hitting scale, early adopter problems, proper plant selection, education and a lack of peer reviewed research.

Grower Ego

I've been in the indoor gardening industry for longer than I want to admit. Just about every grower I have met, minus a specific few, thinks they are the best grower on the planet... period. Growers have bigger egos that anyone and lie more than fishermen! I truly believe this is one of the major obstacles to LED grow light adoption.

Let me be very clear: if you feel compelled to tell people you're the best grower, you're NOT the best grower. The best grower NEVER has to brag about their work as their friends and colleagues do it for them. Also you will never be the best grower on the planet if your only experience is with cannabis. Growing other crops bring valuable insights that you will never glean if you simply do the same thing: grow cannabis over and over. If you can't name your favorite varieties of tomatoes, watermelons or corn then you're NOT the best grower.

I hear it all the time: a grower proclaims that they have 20 years of growing experience. To be honest, when I hear this, I start asking this "seasoned grower" what I believe to be simple questions. In all the years, I have yet to have even one grower get all the answers right, many growers missing even the easiest ones. That's when it becomes clear: they've had one year experience twenty times!

Making matters worse are those silly "Master Grower" certification programs. Someone who may have never picked up a shovel in their life can pass a test and proclaim to a gardening expert–hilarious.

Gardening, especially indoors, is a lifelong pursuit. No one can learn everything about gardening from a class or a single growing season, or from five classes and five growing seasons. I tell new growers if they practice good techniques, experiment with purpose and take good notes, in five years they may be able to ask their first good gardening question.

LED Emitters Nearly Reaching Scale

The main reason LED grow lights cost so much is the price of the LEDs themselves, normally called LED "emitters" or "chips". LED manufacturing is analogous to computer chip manufacturing. Remember how expensive personal computers were when they were first introduced? That's because the chips were expensive to manufacture. The manufacturing process for LED emitters is expensive, and it produces a wide range of emitter quality levels from batch to batch. Only a small number of LED emitters produced using current processes are top quality and thus demand top dollar.

The good news for us indoor gardeners is that the price of LED emitters is decreasing rapidly. Globally, tons of money is being spent on LED research that is driving better, more cost-efficient manufacturing and lower costs for higher-quality emitters. Just look around: suddenly every light source is changing to LEDs. From traffic control lights to streetlights, stadium lights, cop cars, household light bulbs and holiday lights, LEDs are spreading like wildfire. Growing demand for LEDs gives LED manufacturers serious incentives to reduce costs and capture a growing share of this market. Indoor gardeners will benefit from this rising tide, with respect to both LED grow light cost and quality.

This is one area that has significantly changed since I published the first edition of this book. Today, there are more LED emitter manufacturers with improved processes allowing LEDs to reach scale. This will continue to drive the cost of the emitters down, making LED grow lights less expensive.

Early Adopter Problems

The "early adopters" are also very much to blame in hindering the spread of LED grow lights, even though this was opposite their intent. Many early adopters, some of whom built their own LED grow lights, posted the results of their experiments online.

With a few notable exceptions, online pictures of early LED grows were quite unappealing: poor-quality photos of scraggly plants that chilled grower interest in LED grow lights. It seems these growers fell into the trap of believing that hanging a new light would improve their garden, instead of focusing on improving their gardening skills and adapting their techniques to their new garden light source.

Plant Selection

There is a lot of genetic variation between plants even within the same species. For example, tomato plants range from small, bush-like plants you would grow in a container on your patio, to large indeterminate vines that can sprawl all over in a sunny spot in good old mother earth. The grower's goals and growing conditions determine which variety will be selected.

Indoor gardeners have been growing under HID grow lights for decades. They have selected the specific plants (genotype and phenotype, more on this in Chapter 6) that meet their goals under those lights. Since LED grow lights are still in their infancy, growers have not yet selected which plants perform better under LED grow lights.

Don't get me wrong, LEDs certainly do an excellent job at growing today's genetics. I am just pointing out that there is a massive opportunity here. Paring proper genetics with proper LED grow lights will be a game changer and <u>is</u> the golden road to extreme harvests.

Education

The biggest reason LED grow lights aren't used more is the lack of this book! Ok that is a bit of a joke but there is some truth to it. No quality educational materials currently exist to help gardeners understand how to adjust their gardening style to work with LED grow lights.

When searching online, if you are able to find anything that is not chock full of errors, spelling mistakes and incorrect use of plant lighting terminology, it has a sales pitch associated with it. Unfortunately only LED grow light manufacturers are developing LED grow light content, and many of them are doing a very bad job.

One the most difficult concepts to get across to indoor gardeners is that any time you make one change in your garden, you will have to make other changes as well. Your garden is a living ecosystem: one change can upset the status quo and lead to other changes. A "change" includes switching to a different growing media, changing nutrients, installing a new light, or changing a ventilation fan.

Switching to LED grow lights is a major garden change, yet many gardeners don't recognize it as such. The "simple" action of replacing HID grow lights with an LED grow lights prompts the need to reexamine everything about garden setup and practice. If you're currently gardening with HIDs, the methods you're currently using in your garden may not work with LED grow lights.

For example, LED grow lights produces less heat: do you need a different air handling strategy? Cooler temperatures will reduce the level of evaporation: do you need to revise your watering schedule or switch to a growing media that retains less moisture? Did your humidity go up or down as a result these changes? If so, you may need to think more creatively about ventilation.

Now is the time to open your eyes and tune into your plants. They will tell you everything you need to know if you are able to understand them. Even if you're an experienced gardener, when you switch to LED grow lights, think of yourself as a rookie grower again and pay close attention to how your actions affect your garden. Over a few harvests, you'll develop you own technique and soon be overgrowing the planet. Again, you can't learn everything you need to know from a single grow. This is normal and to be expected.

This book gives you a framework for selecting the proper LED grow light for the type of growing you want to do, plus techniques that will help you succeed. LED grow lights are wonderful indoor garden tools, and some day they will hang in <u>every</u> indoor garden. This book will help you unlock the mysteries, challenge the myths, and make LED grow lights work for you.

Lack of Peer Reviewed Research

One of the largest problems holding the entire cannabis industry back is the lack of actual scientific research. There is almost no peer reviewed cannabis research being conducted today. There are many "experts" making claims after they tried it once. Sorry but one single trial does not prove anything. In science you have to run the experiment over and over to make sure you're not seeing a fluke. This sample size can be quite large with dozens to hundreds of repeated trials. Once this initial research is completed it needs to be reproduced by multiple teams located in different parts of the world. If those teams come up with the same results, then and only then can you say you have discovered something.

Most cannabis "research" is anecdotal at best. You can't blindly take research conducted on other crops and say it works on cannabis. Just because some experimental protocol works for Arabidopsis does not automatically mean it's going to apply to cannabis. I see people making this mistake far too often.

One of my personal goals is to open a world class cannabis research institute and do my part to unlock the mysteries of the cannabis plant. I've got an ever growing list of experiments to conduct. If anyone reading this book has a big bunch of money to give to me to establish the American Cannabis Research Institute of America (ACRIA), get in touch!

3: Photosynthesis and Photomorphogenesis

Now that we've covered lighting terminology and why LED grow lights matter, there's one more set of concepts we need to dig into before getting to the "meat" about LED grow lights and how to use them: photosynthesis and photomorphogenesis. These plant processes are the "why" of garden lighting, the key plant biological processes that grow lights are designed to optimize. You need to have a basic understanding of these processes, and how light affects them, in order to know what to look for in a grow light—any grow light—including an LED.

Photosynthesis

Stated simply, photosynthesis is the process by which plants convert light energy into the carbohydrates they use as building blocks and energy stores. Light absorbing pigments in plants do the heavy lifting, collecting light energy and passing it along to chemical processes inside the leaves that convert light, water, and carbon dioxide (CO_2) into carbohydrates. The overall reaction looks like this:

$$\text{Water } (H_2O) + \text{light } (hv) + \text{Carbon Dioxide } (CO_2) \rightarrow \text{Carbohydrates} + \text{Oxygen } (O_2)$$

Photosynthesis can be broken down into two sub-processes: light-dependent reactions and light-independent reactions. It might be simpler to consider the light-dependent reactions "water side" reactions because they use light energy to break up a water molecule (H_2O). The energy produced from these reactions is captured in two compounds that fuel the rest of the photosynthetic process: ATP (adenosine triphosphate) and NADPH (nicotinamide adenine dinucleotide phosphate). Below is the simplified light-dependent/water side reaction:

$$H_2O + \text{light} \rightarrow ATP + NADPH + O_2$$

"Light-independent reactions" are more commonly called "dark reactions," though they don't only occur at night as their name might imply. They just don't require light, so it's better to call them light-independent reactions.

In these reactions, CO_2 is converted into carbohydrates with the aid of the energy building blocks produced by the light-dependent reactions, ATP and NADPH. Because these reactions consume CO_2, they can be considered "carbon fixation" reactions. Simplified, the light independent/carbon fixation reaction looks like this:

 **EXPERT CORNER**

Light-independent reactions are also called the "Calvin Cycle". Melvin Calvin, James Bassham, and Andrew Benson discovered it while working together at University of California, Berkeley, but Calvin gets the name recognition.

$$ATP + NADPH + CO_2 \rightarrow \text{Carbohydrates} + O_2$$

Placing both simplified halves together we get:

Light-Dependent Cycle: H_2O + light → ATP + NADPH + O_2
Light-Independent Cycle: <u>ATP + NADPH + CO_2</u> → Carbohydrates
Total Two-Step Reaction: H_2O + light + CO_2 → Carbohydrates + O_2

Chlorophylls

Chlorophylls are probably the best-known group of plant pigments. They are green in color and found in all plants and algae. Chlorophylls, being the main photoreceptors, are essential for photosynthesis as it's their job is to absorb energy from the photons to which the plant is exposed.

Green plants use both chlorophyll A and chlorophyll B to capture light for photosynthesis. There are also C1, C2, D, and F chlorophylls, but these are generally found in lower plant forms such as algae and diatoms.

In plants, chlorophylls absorb strongly in the red and blue regions of visible light and slightly less in the green region. This is how we wound up with burple LED grow lights–simply trying to stimulate just chlorophylls. Energy savings from producing "only the wavelengths that drive photosynthesis" was a benefit touted by early LED grow light manufacturers and enthusiasts, including me in my October 2008 Growing Edge International magazine article "Close Encounters of the LED Kind". Unfortunately, none of us saw the plant lighting big picture at the time. Now we appreciate green.

This leads to a <u>critically</u> important fact about photosynthesis. <u>Any</u> photon absorbed by photosynthetic pigments in the plant, regardless of wavelength, drives photosynthesis exactly the same. Although some LED grow light manufacturers will argue this fact, it is true. This should make sense: all the photons chlorophyll captures ultimately become deexcited to the energy state of photons captured on the red side of chlorophyll A before heading off to perform photosynthesis. In other words, plants use all the photons they absorb for photosynthetic work, but they need to convert the non-red ones to red before further processing via photosynthesis.

One curiosity about chlorophyll is its close resemblance to hemoglobin, the human molecule that provides oxygen and carbon dioxide transport throughout the body. The primary difference between chlorophyll and hemoglobin is their center ion: hemoglobin centers on iron (Fe), while chlorophyll centers on magnesium (Mg). Otherwise, the molecules are strikingly similar.

RuBisCO

Ribulose-1,5-bisphosphate carboxylase/oxygenase (RuBisCO) is an enzyme involved in the first major step in the light-independent/carbon fixation stage of photosynthesis. RuBisCO enables a plant to capture carbon for further processing into carbohydrates by lowering the energy needed to bind atmospheric CO_2.

As far as enzymes go, RuBisCO is inefficient. It only fixes 1-12 molecules of CO_2 per second in most plants. Many other enzymes "cycle" hundreds to millions of times per second. RuBisCO's low efficiency rate is a major limiting factor in the photosynthetic rate. Keeping the RuBisCO wheel turning is critical to growing large plants.

Fun Fact

RuBisCO is the most abundant protein in plant leaves. It accounts for 50% of soluble protein in C3 plant leaves and 30% in C4 plant leaves. (More on plant types in Chapter 6)

Before RuBisCO can perform its function, it needs to be activated. The first step in RuBisCO activation is completed by an organic molecule called RuBisCO Activase. When RuBisCO is initially formed, it gets immediately locked up with sugars that inhibit its function. RuBisCO Activase removes the inhibiting sugar complex. The last step activating RuBisCO is the attachment of a magnesium ion (Mg^{2+}). Once that is complete, RuBisCO is ready to perform its enzymatic work.

After activation, RuBisCO enables the reaction between ribulose-1,5-bisphosphate (RuBP) and CO_2. This results in fixing a single molecule of carbon per reaction which then can be used to create carbohydrates. It takes six carbons to make a single sugar molecule, another reason why photosynthesis is very inefficient!

RuBisCO:sugar + RuBisCO activase → RuBisCO + Mg → RuBisCO:Mg + CO_2 → carbohydrates

Enzymes and Temperature

Enzymes are proteins that only function when they are physically in their proper three-dimensional shape. If they are structurally off even a little bit they don't work. Think of a lock and a key – although there are many other similar keys only the exact shaped one will unlock the lock. The shape needs to be perfect or the enzyme can't do its job.

Enzymes only operate within specific temperature ranges. In order for them to bend into the proper shape, they need to be flexible. The low end of the optimum temperature range reduces flexibility causing a slowdown in enzyme efficiency. It simply takes longer to achieve the correct shape. Outside the optimum temperature range and the enzyme will be too rigid to function at all. This is why leaf surface temperature is so critical—a few degrees outside the optimal range creates a MAJOR slowdown in the photosynthetic rate, which means fewer carbons are being fixed, fewer carbohydrates created, and a slower growth rate.

The moral of the RuBisCO story is this: without the availability of a few enzymes, proper temperatures, and available magnesium, photosynthesis slows way down. This is why you MUST monitor leaf surface temperatures in your grow, NOT room temperatures.

Leaf Surface Temperature

The best way to understand leaf temperatures, aka "what the plants are feeling", is to use an infrared temperature gun to take multiple measurements in different parts of the grow room and different parts of the plants. Observe temperatures throughout your grow space and pay attention to variations between readings.

Temperatures will naturally be higher near the top of the garden and lower near the bottom since heat rises. If you discover hot or cold spots at the same "altitude", such as between plants that stand right next to each other, you may have discovered areas that are not getting sufficient air movement. Try moving the plants around or changing fan locations to even out the temperatures.

I've worked with many commercial HID growers that were trialing LED grow lights and completely failed. Their number one mistake was not increasing the leaf surface temperatures of their gardens. They were too scared to warm up the room to allow for proper leaf surface temperatures based on their previous HID experience where heat was always the enemy. The conversation is always the same: reluctantly they increase the set point on their A/C which raises the grow room temperature, and then they see immediate results. I usually get a call back within a day or two, stating the garden is looking much better and they just should have listened in the first place. What have they done? Enabled RuBisCO to do its job!

For cannabis, a leaf surface temperature of 75°F/24°C is NOT going to cut it. RuBisCO activity will be very limited and that will dramatically affect the growth rate of the garden. Get over it and increase your temperatures! Cannabis leaf surface temperature should be 80-82°F/27-28°C. More on proper environmental conditions in chapter 6.

Leaf vs. Wall Temperature

Measuring garden temperatures accurately is not as easy as it seems. Be suspicious when someone brags that his or her garden stays a perfect 82°F/28°C all the time—how do they know? Most gardeners depend on a combination thermometer/hygrometer placed somewhere in the garden, which measures both temperature and relative humidity. Many also record high and low values. Elite gardeners use devices that provide a 24-hour recording of temperatures and humidity. All of these gardeners believe that their recording sensors tell them exactly what's happening in their gardens—but do they?

In a word, *no*. Most garden temperature devices are hung on the wall or receive input from a long-wired sensor that's suspended over the garden in a single spot. Moving that sensor up and down a few inches to a foot will change the measurement, possibly by quite a bit. If you're using one of these sensors, try moving it six inches in any direction—the results may surprise you. It's almost as though you should ask yourself: what temperature do you want it to read?

While a temperature/humidity monitor can provide a good *indication* of what's happening in the garden, there's a lot more to the story. The temperature at the wall can vary significantly from the temperature of the plants' leaves. Leaf temperature is what really matters.

Carotenoids

The second most abundant class of plant light-harvesting compounds are called carotenoids (aka carotenes). They are typically yellow and orange and occasionally red in color. In the fall when the tree leaves change, carotenoids are responsible for the varying colors as the chlorophylls fade away.

Carotenes are responsible for the colors of many fruits and vegetables such as carrots and corn. β-carotene and lycopene are the most commonly known carotenoids.

 Fun Fact

It's not just plants that synthesize carotenoids. Both spider mites and aphids are also capable. They inherited the necessary genes from fungi.

Green Light

Green light has gotten a bad rap when it comes to photosynthesis. We've been told since we were children that plants look green to our eyes because they reflect green light. While that's partially true, plants don't reflect 100% of the green light they receive–some is absorbed and some is reflected. Many plants absorb as much as 70% to 90% of the green light to which they are exposed. Reflected green light can be absorbed by another leaf increasing the chance that green light will get absorbed. Because of reflection, green light scatters further into the garden's canopy than red or blue.

Green light is absorbed deep within the leaf tissue by carotenoids. Carotenoids cause plant leaves to thicken, increasing their ability to capture more light. Also, plants have mechanisms to shut down red/blue absorption while in defense mode against excess heat or light, while allowing green to continue absorption to fuel themselves. Green light is looking better, huh?

Another good reason for green in your LED grow light is to make using it easier on your eyes. Red, blue, and green are the primary colors of light: when they are mixed together in computer monitors and televisions, they can recreate every color including white. Including green in an LED grow light makes it easier for the gardener to see problems that might otherwise be masked by unsafe burple.

Emerson Enhancement Effect

In 1957, Robert Emerson conducted experiments regarding what wavelengths most efficiently drive photosynthesis. He noticed that photosynthesis dramatically drops off at 680nm and above. This was considered strange since chlorophyll isolated in a beaker absorbs light well above this point. Photosynthesis reductions above 680nm became known as the "red drop effect".

This led Emerson to additional experiments showing that plants respond disproportionately to the combination of far-red light and red wavelengths. He observed a dramatic increase in photosynthetic rates when the plants he tested were exposed to red and far-red light at the same time. This phenomenon became known as the "Emerson Enhancement Effect".

There is limited crop specific research on the multiplying effect that Emerson's results indicate and none includes cannabis. Specific trials on cannabis need to be conducted to know for sure. This is one topic that I would personally like to research.

Photosystem I and Photosystem II

Emerson's body of work was groundbreaking at the time. He was responsible for discovering both Photosystem I (PSI) and Photosystem II (PSII). PSI and PSII have two different jobs to perform within the light-dependent phase of photosynthesis.

PSII is actually considered to be the first step in in photosynthesis, although it was discovered after PSI and so named PSII. PSII's job is to oxidize water (H_2O) into oxygen (O_2), 4 protons and 4 electrons ($2 H_2O \rightarrow O_2 + 4H^+ + 4e^-$). PSI function is to reduce $NADP^+$ into NADPH ($NADP^+ + H^+ + 2e^- \rightarrow NADPH$).

What if Emerson had it Backwards?

This leads me to a new theory (or at least I have not seen it published yet) that there is no "enhancement effect" at all. Thinking about it differently, what if red and far-rod are required for complete photosynthesis stimulation? Instead of "enhancing" by adding far-red light, it could be that adding far-red light corrects a deficiency that hinders photosynthesis. It could be that the difference associated with the Emerson Enhancement Effect is the "cost" of less efficient photosynthesis when far-red is missing. Since natural sunlight contains both red and far-red, it makes sense that the effect was "discovered" once we started manipulating plant lighting indoors. Ahh science!

Far-Red

More importantly, far-red has a significant morphological effects on plants, that is, it effects a plant's structure and shape. Plants that have been exposed to far-red often show an increase in leaf area, making a plant capable of absorbing more photons and potentially growing more. This can be an advantage for plants that don't flower, such as lettuce, to increase overall yield. Far-red light is another area that needs more research.

There can be problems with far-red though, especially for flowering plants. Far-red exposure can increase internodal distances, which results in taller plants–not typically what an indoor gardener wants. This is a shade avoidance technique developed by plants. Plants do not absorb all the far-red light they are exposed to but they do soak up just about all of the red. When a plant receives a disproportionately high amount of far-red it thinks it's being blocked by another plant that's grabbing up all the red. Its response is to grow taller so it too can have red light.

Photosynthetic Efficiency

Did you know that photosynthesis is only about 1-4% efficient in most plants? This means that only a few of every hundred photons that are absorbed by the plant are actually used in photosynthesis. The rest are given off through various mechanisms, quite a bit of it as heat.

This inefficiency has led to some interesting experiments, such as one that postulated since plants only use a small fraction of the light they are exposed to, why not flash the lights? It sounds like a good idea on the surface but it does not work that way. Flashing on and off for equal durations would definitely cut electric consumption but unfortunately photosynthesis is also decreased at the same rate. Since our goal is to fix as many carbon molecules as possible in a day, flashing the lights is not a winning strategy.

Originally it was thought that low photosynthetic efficiency was due to slow transfer of energy between the light-dependent and the light-independent reactions. It turns out that the rate of this reaction is so fast you can't flash the lights fast enough to make a difference.

Photomorphogenesis

Understanding what light wavelengths you need in an LED grow light can be a daunting task. Typical photosynthesis charts show the chlorophyll response curve at each wavelength within PAR spectrum, with some giving consideration to what is absorbed by the various carotenoids. But there is more to the picture: light spectra outside the PAR range, commonly called signaling wavelengths, are also needed for healthy plant growth. Signaling wavelengths regulate plant growth and development such as controlling internodal stretching. The impact of light on plant shape and structure is called photomorphogenesis.

Phytochrome

Phytochrome is an extremely important plant growth regulator that functions in the red end of the visible light spectrum. While it has no role in photosynthesis, phytochrome controls internodal elongation and a plant's ability to measure day length (photoperiodism). The best understood of the plant-signaling compounds, phytochrome has two active states: phytochrome red (P_r) absorbs light from ~650nm to 670nm, and phytochrome far-red (P_{fr}) absorbs light at ~705nm to 740nm. Note that the P_{fr} absorption is outside of the PAR spectrum range.

The ratio between P_r and P_{fr}, which convert back and forth depending on the light the plant receives, affects the plant's physical shape including its height. Plants use phytochrome to sense the amount of red and far-red light they are receiving. As mentioned before, without enough red light, the plants will sense that they are being blocked from the light and will stretch (increase internodal distance) to search for it.

Short-day plants (more on plant types in Chapter 6) also rely on phytochrome to initiate flowering. Flowering begins when a sufficient quantity of P_{fr} converts back to the P_r form, a process that requires about 12 hours of uninterrupted darkness. That's why short-day plants grown outdoors begin to flower when day lengths shorten after summer solstice, and why indoor growers switch to a 12-hours-on/12-hours-off light cycle for flowering short-day plants such as cannabis.

On the research front, growers have been experimenting with phytochrome to extend "day" length during the flowering phase. Why lengthen the day? So that your plants have more time to turn light into carbohydrates and then use those carbohydrates to grow stronger stems and bigger yields. Growers have been able to increase yields by keeping the lights on for 13 or 14 hours then finishing the light cycle with far-red light only for periods ranging from a few seconds to a few minutes. This short period of far-red light jumpstarts the P_{fr}-to-P_r conversion process, allowing the plants to convert enough P_{fr} to P_r during a shortened night cycle to continue vigorous flowering.

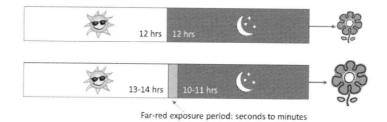

Far-red exposure period: seconds to minutes

Some growers also report that this process allows them to grow the same-sized plants but harvest their crop a few days to weeks sooner than without the far-red exposure at lights out. Personally I have not seen any actual garden successfully deploy this technique.

Phytochrome Photostationary State

The Phytochrome Photostationary State (PPS) describes the ratio of red to far-red light. In this metric, red light is defined from 640-680nm and far-red light is from 710-750nm. The PSS metric was Introduced by Sager et al. in 1998. As reference, sunlight is calculated at 0.7 while shade under a tightly closed canopy can have a PPS as low as 0.1. When PPS values drop too low, the plant thinks it is in the shade and stretches. If you have detailed output data down to the nanometer level of a grow fixture, you can calculate PPS as follows:

$$PSS = \frac{Pr}{Pr + Pfr}$$

Far-Red vs. Infrared

There is a surprising amount of misinformation regarding the wavelengths just above the red region. I myself have misquoted the difference between far-red and infrared, so I thought I would shed some light on the topic (pun intended). Red is fairly easy–it's emitted from approximately 630 to 700nm.

The next band up is the far-red region and where some disagreement exists. Photobiologists typically agree the far-red region covers ~700-780nm, while physicists consider the region to be closer to ~700-750nm. Then there's the infrared region. Infrared is massive when compared to the visible portion of light. It starts at 780nm (or 750nm) and continues to million nanometers.

I've seen many LED grow lights advertised as containing "infrared light" because they include 735nm emitters. No matter what your point of view, 735nm is far-red not infrared. Maybe this is not a huge point, but it does show a lack of understanding of light science on the part of certain LED grow light manufacturers. Have some fun… quiz the LED lighting manufacturers about far-red and infrared in their lights and see how much they know!

Cryptochrome

Cryptochrome is a photosensor similar to phytochrome, though it captures blue, violet and a small amount of UV-A light. While less understood than phytochrome, cryptochrome also assists in regulating the physical size and shape of plants, both alone and in combination with phytochrome.

Cryptochrome affects the plant's "circadian clock," which is how the plant perceives night and day, as well as being responsible for **phototropism**–the process that causes plants to turn toward the light. Sunflowers provide an example of phototropism: in most varieties their flowers track the sun from the east in the morning to the west in the evening.

It's not necessary to buy an LED grow light with UV-A spectrum to activate cryptochrome, in fact, it's safer for your eyes and skin if you don't. Most current LED grow lights have sufficient blue light to activate cryptochrome photosensors without added UV light.

Phototropins

Phototropins are blue-light receptors that control a range of responses that optimize the photosynthetic efficiency of plants. These include phototropism, light-induced stomatal opening, and chloroplast movements in response to changes in light intensity. In addition, phototropins mediate the first changes in stem elongation in blue light prior to cryptochrome activation.

UV Light

There are three bands of UV light: UV-A, UV-B, and UV-C. Each has different characteristics, applications and hazards. The following table explains the differences:

	Wavelength	Applications	Other
UV-A	320–400nm "Long Wave"	Black light	Excites cryptochrome, increases flavonoids
UV-B	280–320nm "Medium Wave"	Reptile lamps, Phototherapy	Causes sunburns, reduces powdery mildew and spider mites
UV-C	200–280nm "Short Wave"	Germicidal	Mostly filtered by the atmosphere, harmful

Until recently, the only way to add UV to your garden was through tanning or reptile bulbs. There were some UV LEDs but they very expensive and had very short lifespans. Like everything, technology has moved the performance of UV LEDs forward greatly. UV LEDs are much cheaper today and have significantly increased useful lives. Let the experiments begin!

There is quite a bit of controversy about the effects of UV on cannabis. Some say it increases THC and/or flavonoids others say it does nothing at all. Is it because we've been using the wrong UV types? Have we misapplied the light somehow? I've got new ideas on the topic to share.

Some research suggests that the application of UV should be done at night. Blue light helps activate enzymes that restore damage to internal plant structures including DNA. It is theorized that exposing blue light at the same time as UV mitigates the effect of the UV application. Since UV light falls out of the PAR range, it won't affect the photoperiod if applied at night.

We also might have been applying UV when not needed. If the current theories prove true, UV supplementation is only helpful for a few hours a night for the last few weeks of flower. This is when cannabis plants are producing the majority of the cannabinoids, flavonoids and terpenes which UV is suspected to stimulate.

Which UV?

There are a bunch of conflicting theories about which wavelengths of UV are beneficial to the cannabis plant. Some say it's UV-A all the way. Others swear UV-B is the better choice. To be perfectly honest, everyone is guessing right now as there has not been any peer-reviewed, science-based testing of UV on cannabis plants. It's most likely going to be a combination of both UV-A and UV-B. I think we will also find different light recipes for different plant genotypes and phenotypes.

EXPERT CORNER

UV-B radiation is captured via the UV-B photoreceptor UV resistance locus 8 (UVR8).

UV-A

UV-A stimulates cryptochrome and phototropins. These two photoreceptors regulate various physiological and developmental processes including elongation, germination, chloroplast relocation, and stomatal opening. Proper stomatal regulation is critical for water transpiration and CO_2 exchange. Additionally, UV-A has been shown to increase flavonoids in some plants.

UV-B

Some recent trials seem to show that UV-B increases THC production. UV-B stress is believed to stimulate cannabis's production of a chemical called malonyl-CoA. Cannabis uses malonyl-CoA to make Olivetolic acid, which is a precursor to further cannabinoid production. Olivetolic acid when combined with geranyl diphosphate (GPP) creates cannabigerolic acid (CBGa), the precursor to both THCa and CBDa.

One interesting thing to note is that there have not been any increases in CBD production in these UV-B trials. It seems that UV-B is stimulating the THCa synthase but not CBDa synthase. A lot more research needs to be done on this subject.

A word of caution: there is a lot of energy in the UV-B portion of the electromagnetic spectrum. Make sure to protect your skin and eyes if working with a grow fixture that emits photons in this region. This should not be a problem if you're running your UV exposure during the dark period.

UV and Pest Control

What if two of the most common pest pressures in a grow facility could be solved with light? Early findings show that very low levels of ~285nm photons (at the bottom end of UV-B region) at less than 1 PFD can reduce and/or eliminate powdery mildew. Slightly higher photon densities at about 1 PFD have been shown to kill and/or drive off spider mites. Since spider mites typically live on the undersides of leaves, the UV light would have to be somehow bounced off the grow table. The exact target wavelengths and durations need to be worked out. This is another area of research to keep an eye on.

Another reason to consider UV is it can be used at the end of a grow cycle to help sanitize the room. After the harvest, the UV could be left on overnight at elevated levels to help kill off any mites and molds. This UV treatment would be in addition to normal post-harvest cleaning procedures.

The McCree Curve

Keith J. McCree was a professor of soil and crop sciences at Texas A&M University in the early 1970s. He conducted experiments to determine what wavelength(s) drive photosynthesis with the highest efficiency. This work got summarized into a chart that's referred to as "The McCree Curve".

Many cannabis growers reference the McCree Curve as the definitive proof of how plants and light interact. Unfortunately there are some major problems with his study. The first problem is the study included only 22 different crops and cannabis was not one of them. The second problem is that the study measured single leaves, under low light exposures–not the whole plant. It's theorized that the whole plant might behave differently. The third problem is there is no way know how the results translate to desired characteristics such as yield, visual appearance, or extractible oils.

McCree was faced was the limited availability of lighting technology in the 1970s. He used broad-spectrum light sources (HIDs) and colored filters to obtain the wavelengths in which he exposed to the test plant leaf. The good news is that with the modern high-powered LED grow lights we have today, this research can continue and build on what he started.

Daily Light Integral

The Daily Light Integral (DLI) is the total amount of PAR received by a plant during a single photoperiod. DLI is expressed in units of moles per meter squared per day (mol m^{-2} day^{-1}). DLI is simply taking PPFD measurements every second during a 24-hour day and adding them up. Greenhouse growers can purchase PPFD loggers that automate the process. Calculating DLI is easy. For indoor growers, it's as simple as taking an average PPFD reading and doing some math. PPFD measurements only needs to be done once a day since the light intensity does not typically change over a day. Additionally, there are quite a few DLI calculators available online if math is not your strong point. All you need is your PPFD readings and photoperiod length to use one.

Use the equation below to calculate the DLI generated by your grow light. This example assumes a grow light that provides a PPFD of 1,400 µmol m^{-2} sec^{-1} during a 12-hour photoperiod:

$$\left(\frac{1,400\ \mu mol}{m^2 \cdot sec}\right) * \left(\frac{60\ sec}{min}\right) * \left(\frac{60\ min}{hour}\right) * \left(\frac{12\ hour}{day}\right) * \left(\frac{1\ mol}{1,000,000\ \mu mol}\right)$$

$$= \frac{60.4\ mol}{m^2 \cdot day}$$

For reference, the maximum DLI that can be achieved outside in full summer sun is about 65 moles/day. For most crops this level should not be exceeded. Many commercially grown plants have published DLI ranges. On the next page is a short list of DLI's for common plants:

Crop Type	mol m^{-2} day^{-1}
Small herbs	10-12
Lettuce	14-16
Peppers	20-30
Tomatoes	22-30
Cannabis Full Flower	TBD

There is very limited amount of cannabis-specific research regarding its maximum DLI but plenty of strong opinions. Be wary of anyone, especially LED grow light manufacturers, that make specific claims of a maximum cannabis DLI, especially if it coincidentally matches the upper end of the performance of the lights they are trying to sell. The truth is they don't know. No one knows. I am not aware of any peer-reviewed studies conducted into the maximum DLI for cannabis at this time.

To drive this point home, many years ago I saw a garden with over 4,000 watts of HPS per 4x8 tray just prior to harvest. Although I did not have a quantum sensor and meter to measure the actual PPFD, it topped out my Lux meter at the canopy level. Based on a conversion, the meter's cut off point was about ~2000 µmol m^{-2} s^{-1} (which is a DLI of greater than 86 mol m^{-2} day^{-1}).

The grow was MASSIVE. This grow showed me that the cannabis plant can take considerably more light intensities that anyone is currently delivering. Some might call this example electrically inefficient. All I can say is they didn't see it! With the next generation of LED grow lights, every garden will harvest like that one or better.

In my experience from taking PPFD readings in commercial grow facilities, I rarely see PPFD levels above 750-800 µmol m^{-2} s^{-1} delivered to the canopy. That is significantly lower than a cannabis plant can use. Anyone who has grown outside under the "big bulb in the sky" knows that cannabis can handle more. PPFD levels during summer days can reach ~2000 µmol m^{-2} s^{-1}, more than double average indoor grow light levels. In short, most cannabis producers are limiting their potential harvest at their current light levels.

Working with DLI: DLI Maintenance

I have realized there is an important topic that is not currently being discussed in the industry–"DLI maintenance", which I define as the need to maintain the DLI when we transition from vegetative to flowering stages. Let's say we veg our plants at 600 PPFD for 18 hours per day for a DLI of 38.8 mol m^{-2} day^{-1}. To maintain the same DLI after changing to 12 hours of light per day, we would need to increase the PPFD to 900.

The reality is most plants won't handle that large of a jump in one day. It's up to you to learn how much your plants can handle during the transition. The main reason to maintain the DLI is to lessen transitional stress on short-day plants, not add more! Healthy cannabis plants typically can handle splitting the difference and ramping up light the levels over a week or two. Using the example above, the when transitioning from 600 PPFD, start by increasing the PPFD to 750 and increase 25-50 µmol m^{-2} s^{-1} a day until your reach your target level.

A good question to ask is why have we not been discussing DLI maintenance until now? The answer is that we simply didn't have this problem before LEDs. When growing with HIDs, the DLI maintenance problem basically resolves itself since the metal halide lamps typically used to veg plants produce less photons for the same energy as the HPS lamps typically used for flowering. Assuming the grower uses similar light heights for veg and flower cycles, photon density is automatically increased when the "veg" MH lamp is swapped out for the "flower" HPS lamp.

Photoinhibition

It is possible to exceed the light requirements of our plants with modern LED grow lights, something that rarely if ever happens under HIDs. When exposed to too much light intensity, plants shut down photosynthesis through a process called photoinhibition.

Photoinhibition is a serious problem: not only are the plants not converting light into carbohydrates so they can grow, they are spending energy to defend themselves through a process called "feedback de-excitation" that disperses excess energy from over-stimulated chlorophyll molecules. Unfortunately, feedback de-excitation also releases dangerous free radicals inside the plant, which attack chlorophyll molecules and other structures.

Photorespiration

Photorespiration (also called C_2 photosynthesis) is the process in which plants begin "binding" oxygen (O_2) instead of carbon dioxide (CO_2). Although this process is continually occurring while plants are illuminated, it occurs at a significantly higher rate at high temperatures or at low concentrations of CO_2.

Photorespiration is a wasteful process. Instead of fixing carbon though the Calvin cycle, carbon is actually released by photorespiration–basically the exact opposite of what plants need. To combat the effects of photorespiration, keep your garden within optimal temperatures and CO_2 concentrations.

Photoinhibition is possible because RuBisCO, which drives the light-independent photosynthetic reactions, cannot differentiate between CO_2 and O_2. When RuBisCO can't bind CO_2 (photosynthesis) it binds O_2 (photorespiration). This is where the "C" and the "O" in RuBisCO come from – C for carboxylase when RuBisCO fixing carbon dioxide, and O for oxygenase when it's fixing oxygen.

Photooxidation

Also referred to as "photo-bleaching", **photooxidation** is a fancy way of saying that flowers at the top of the plant are not creating chlorophyll, and thus they are "bleached" white. The white areas are exactly the same as the rest of the green plant with respect to metabolites such as terpenes and cannabinoids, just lacking chlorophylls. Susceptibility to photooxidation is highly individualized–some plants express the condition and some don't, even when they are from the same genotype (phenotype expression).

The latest theory regarding photooxidation is that older generations of LED grow lights contained too much red and not enough blue. While the science on photooxidation in cannabis plants is still being developed, there is good news—we are seeing less of this under broad spectrum white-dominant LED grow lights.

Steve Cantwell, one of the best growers I've ever met, proposed another theory to me. His idea is that photooxidation is linked to temperature. As he increased the leaf surface temperatures, he saw a decrease in bleaching. Warming up your LED grow rooms is looking better and better huh? More research is definitely needed.

4: LED Grow Lights: The Photon

Now at last we come to the matter at hand: understanding and using LED grow lights. The most important aspect of any grow light is the light it produces... duh! This chapter focuses on the light LED grow lights emit, while the next focuses on LED grow light fixtures themselves. Let's begin with a basic question.

What's Different About LED Grow Lights?

LEDs open up a whole new world for indoor gardening. Now we can grow in taller or smaller spaces, control the exact wavelengths of light that reach our plants instead of adapting our gardening methods to what's available from traditional lighting technology, and even create plant-specific lights that are efficient for growing a particular crop if we desire. The operating characteristics of LED grow lights, particularly the fact that they create less heat, change the way we design our gardens and grow facilities.

Less Heat

Why do LEDs produce less heat? It's simple: LED grow lights use less watts–somewhere between 50% to 60% of HID watts. Less watts equals less heat. While explaining heat is a rather complicated topic, ask yourself this: what happens when the light is switched off? The photons of light cease to exist, but what happens to them?

Physics tells us that photons "decay" into the "system," which in this case is the grow room. This phenomenon is described in the theory of conservation of energy, which states that energy cannot be created or destroyed–it can only be converted form one form to another. This is a long way of saying that when light decays, it becomes heat.

 **EXPERT CORNER**

Infrared heaters work by heating exposed surfaces, which in turn heat the surrounding air. This is the opposite of traditional heaters where heated air warms the surfaces. Keep in mind that in your garden, those surfaces being heated are your plants' leaves and stems!

As defined by physics, 1 watt of electricity equals 3.412 British Thermal Units (BTU/h) per hour. This is true for all light sources–HID, fluorescent, LED, or any other electrical appliance: whether it's a light, a power drill or an electric heater it's still 3.412 BTU/h for every watt you're using.

When discussing heat make sure you know who you're talking to. If you're discussing heat loads with a lighting scientist, they will typically calculate the heat from the lights not the total HVAC needs of the garden. Ultimately you will need an HVAC specialist who knows how to make calculations that consider lights, the plants' needs, and effects of the external environment to when designing a proper cooling/dehumidifying system for both summer and winter conditions. Local environmental knowledge is required to get it right.

An additional reason LEDs produce less heat is that HID lamps, especially HPS lamps, produce a lot of waste heat in the infrared region of the light spectrum. Infrared heats the surfaces it comes in contact with and has been used for decades to heat bathrooms and keep food warm in restaurants.

If lamp manufacturers published spectral power distribution (SPD) charts that went beyond the typical end point of 770nm, it would be easier to understand where this extra infrared heat energy comes from. The following chart shows that HPS lights generate a large peak around 810nm-plus, which is all infrared heat—quite a lot, in fact, compared to the PAR emitted.

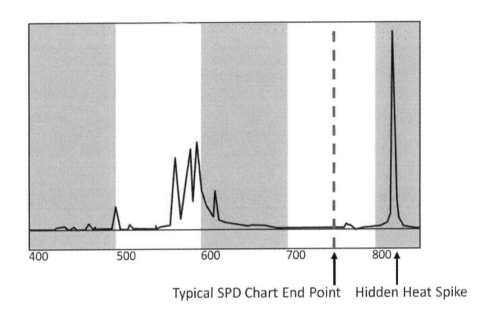

Typical SPD Chart End Point   Hidden Heat Spike

New Spectra Not Available Under HID

Indoor gardeners will attempt to grow with any lighting technology that comes along. Whether fluorescent, metal halide, high-pressure sodium, low-pressure sodium, ceramic metal halide, induction, LED, or plasma, every new lighting technology will eventually take its turn in an indoor gardening trial. All of these lighting technologies except LEDs have the same problem: you're stuck with the spectrum that manufacturer produces, which is limited by the physical properties of the lighting technology itself.

One of the best things about LED grow lights is the ability to control the specific light energy plants receive. Want more blue? If your light allows it, add more blue emitters. If not, supplement with an all-blue LED fixture. If you want more red, add it. Some LED grow light manufacturers will accept special orders for grow lights with custom spectrum colors. If you want to grow with or test a particular spectrum mix in your garden, that's now possible.

Adjustable Spectrum

Some LED grow lights offer the ability to alter the light spectrum they produce. Some are very sophisticated lights which allow independent control of far-red, red, multiple whites, and sometimes UV. They connect to a computer or have on-board controls for customizing their spectral "mix".

The reason to adjust the spectrum is to alter the red-to-blue and red-to-far-red ratios. Through these alterations, growers can induce desired morphological responses within plants. This is done by controlling the specific number of photons that light harvesting complexes such as phytochrome, cryptochrome and phototropins receive at various stages of growth.

My experience with tunable lights came from the second version of the UFO LED grow light that had two separate physical controls for red and blue. For about the first two weeks I monkeyed with the knobs. Like I always say, "give a person a knob and they will turn it"! Each time I went to check the garden something looked funky. The problem was I <u>always</u> left the adjustment knobs in the wrong position <u>every time</u> I touched them. After the first two weeks I turned them both all the way up, duct taped them in place and never looked back.

For this reason I am not a fan of altering the spectrum with physical knobs. Lights with knobs can be successfully deployed in hobby grows if you're very mindful of your changes. Be sure to write down the changes you make. For commercial installs, light spectrum alterations should be controlled by one person and the rest of the crew should not have access. All changes should be logged. This way if you discover something good (or bad), you will know what the setting of the lights were at the time and whether there was a recent change.

Old-timer cannabis growers understand the value of controlling morphological responses through spectral adjustments. Back in the day we veg'd our plants under metal halide and kept our girls under them until flower initiation had begun, typically around week 3. This helped keep our plants shorter due to the high blue-to-red ratio of the halide lamps. Once the stretching period was over, we swapped our halides for high-pressure sodium lamps as the desired morphological responses were done. Since HPS lamps produce quite a bit more PPFD than halides they grew larger flowers.

Adjustable Spectrum and DLI

Most of the current LED grow lights with adjustable spectra make their changes by turning one or more of the color channels down. This is problematic because it decreases DLI, unless you can turn the remaining channels up. There is at least one LED grow manufacturer at the time of the writing of this edition that offers a nearly lossless transition between their light spectra.

There are growers who swear that significantly shifting to blue dominant spectrum (buy turning down the red channel) for the last week will increase terpene/cannabinoid concentrations the final product. Here is my take on the subject—unless you have a properly designed LED grow light, this method literally trades off the plant's carbon fixing process for enhanced production of secondary metabolites. While you <u>might</u> increase terpene and or cannabinoid levels, you will be sacrificing final harvest weight. I guess this choice depends on your goals, but this practice is definitely not supported by adequate science.

Sunrise / Sunset

A current trend in LED grow lights is to add electronic controls to simulate natural processes such as sunrise and sunset. Instead of the lights just turning straight on and off, these lights come on and go off over a short time. I guess the thought is, since "mother nature does it", so should grow lights. Sounds great, but is it?

I personally don't see a need for sunrise but there could be one. Since maximum DLI is critical for heavy harvests, why reduce the amount of light the plants have available to fix carbohydrates during the photoperiod? Let's wake them up and get growing!

Previously I wrote that I didn't see a need for sunset control. I recently heard of a new idea about why sunset could be useful. If you watch humidity levels when the lights turn off you will notice a spike. Controlling the heat load at the end of the day may reduce this effect. When the lights suddenly shut off the temperature of the room drops, which causes the relative humidity of the room to temporarily spike upwards. A slower sunset might help in controlling this humidity.

Which Wavelengths?

Speaking of wavelengths, another question I get asked far too often is which wavelengths should be included in an LED grow light? This is another area where I have changed my thinking. When LED grow lights first appeared, spectral choices were limited to how much red vs. how much blue. As LED grow lights advanced, more wavelengths of light were introduced–this seemed like progress.

This led to a flood of lights with more and more included wavelengths. Suddenly lights with 15 or more discreet, single color emitters were available accompanied by lavish claims of unlocking the magical spectrum to grow plants. Here's the truth: while searching for the perfect spectrum over the years, the LED emitters and drivers themselves gained in efficiency. These newer lights are simply putting more photons on the plants, not unlocking mysteries.

It's Alright to be [Mostly] White

In the last edition I made the prediction that LED grow lights would include full spectrum white LEDs only. In this edition I'm going to change that to "mostly white". There are portions of the electromagnetic spectrum that are useful to plants that are not included in sufficient quantities in white. Mainly these are the red and far-red regions of the electromagnetic spectrum.

Why white? White will win simply because of cost. There is significantly more demand for architectural and general illumination lighting, which typically uses white lights, than for grow lights. Think of it this way–how many street and stadium lights exist compared to grow lights? Therefore, most LED research dollars are focused on improving white emitters, not discrete single colored ones. Ultimately this will drive the development of ever-better white emitters while at the same time reducing their cost.

Why will white work? It's simple: white light works because of its component wavelengths. To make white you'll need a bit of blue, some green, toss in some red and voila–you've got white! Remember any photon, regardless of wavelength, when absorbed by one of the many photosynthetic light absorbing pigments in the plant, drives photosynthesis equally. Red, green, blue or any other color, it doesn't matter as long as those photons are in the PAR range.

We do have to use the correct white emitters though. Although photosynthesis does not care about wavelengths, we still need to drive photomorphogenesis. Based on my experience, having the proper ratios of blue to red and red to far-red is required to stimulate photomorphogenic responses. This is another area that will be changing fast as we collectively learn more.

Plant Light Requirements

The following table, which lists the light wavelengths most commonly absorbed by plants, can be helpful to understand some of their light requirements. For each photo-reactive substance within a plant, the table lists the peak wavelength at which absorption is maximized for that compound's function within the plant.

	Max Absorption Peak(s)
Beta-Carotene	470nm
Chlorophyll A	465nm, 665nm
Chlorophyll B	453nm, 642nm
Phycoerythrin	495 and 545/566nm
Phycocyanin	620nm
Cryptochrome	450nm, 370nm
Phytochrome	P_r 660nm, P_{fr} 730nm

These photoactive compounds will absorb light not only at the listed peak wavelength, but also for some distance on either side of the peak and may also have secondary absorbance peaks. Specific wavelengths are required to stimulate each of the photoactive compounds. In order to react, the wavelength of the photon must equal the difference of the energy between the ground state and the excited state of the compound. This is why each compound has a unique absorbance spectra. With that in mind, it's possible to find broad spectrum LED grow lights with wavelengths that stimulate all of the known photoreceptors.

The simplest way to understand a particular grow light's output is to obtain a **spectral power distribution (SPD)** chart from the manufacturer, such as the one below. An SPD chart provides a visual representation of the light's output to help you to see whether it will suit your garden's needs.

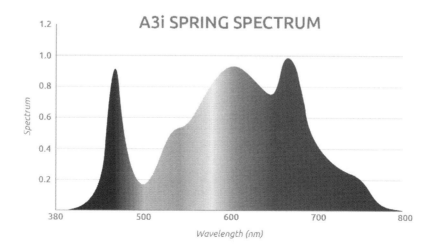

Creating the "Perfect Mix"

The perfect wavelength ratios for growing plants have not been developed yet. The most probable outcome is that these are crop (and potentially phenotype) dependent. The science behind photosynthesis and photomorphogenesis is far from complete, and much of the information included in this book is newly discovered. It's quite possible that there are additional light-harvesting complexes in plants that are not known; we may need different wavelengths or ratios to excite them.

LED research is unlocking new mysteries all the time. There are always new theories and manufacturers willing to build new lights based on them. Time will tell what works and what doesn't. Regardless if you're a hobby or commercial grower, you will need a light that strongly drives both photosynthesis and positively contributes to desired photomorphogenic responses.

Grow Light Myths

One of the things that is most interesting to me is how the hydroponics side of the indoor gardening industry got its start. The original hydroponics pioneers were, for the most part, West Coast hippies figuring out how to grow their own. Or their friends, helping these hippies grow better with improved lighting, stabilized nutrients, growing systems and other equipment.

Thus the "hydroponics" industry was born. Hardware stores wanted nothing to do with this market, so the industry was able to thrive and produce a stream of innovative indoor gardening products without fear of the big box stores stamping it out.

While hydroponics products are effective at growing plants indoors, many of them are based on let's-call-it-less-than "institutional quality" science and research. Until recently, there was not even one photobiologist in the mix. When I chucked my corporate career aside in 2006 to open the first hydroponics shop in Compton, CA, I was one of a few MBAs in the U.S. hydroponic industry.

Along the way, hydroponics pioneers took materials that were available, tested their application in indoor gardening, and figured out what works. Setting aside the chemists who formulate hydroponic nutrients, much of the rest of industry bases product designs on anecdotal factors (e.g., what works, usually in too-short experiments) and simple measurements such as the lumens emitted by an HID lamp.

The lack of rigorous, science-based testing of many hydroponics products, including garden lighting, has created a tolerance for inflated product claims and certain "myths". This is changing fast as budgets and talent improve.

Before they completely disappear, let's bust a few of the myths that are still floating around... how 'bout it?

Two myths in one! Summer-to-Winter Kelvin Shift and Flowering Initiation

MYTH A well-respected garden writer once wrote the following in a popular indoor gardening magazine: "The [high-pressure] sodium light is very red and mimics the fall sun to induce flowering". HID lamp salesmen and hydro shop owners also claim that MH lamps are best for vegetative growth because they are "blue" like spring sunlight while HPS lamps are best for flowering because they resemble "red" fall light. All of this "spring blue" and "fall red" talk is bunk and it incorporates two myths in one: first, that changing light color induces flowering (it doesn't) and that spring and fall daylight are different colors (they are not).

With respect to flowering, we have already discussed how many plants respond to changes in photoperiod (day length) such as flowers that bloom in spring (longer day length) or fall (shorter day length). A lot of plants are photoperiod neutral when it comes to flowering.

With respect to a summer-to-winter daylight color shift, ask yourself this: at midday, does a spring day look blue to you or a fall day look red? In a word, *no*. Light "color" as perceived by humans is measured according to the Kelvin (K) scale with blue having higher values and red lower ones. The world would look very strange indeed if the light temperature of sunlight changed from season to season by anything even close to the 2000-2500K difference between MH and HPS lamps.

Don't misunderstand: there *is* a seasonal shift in daylight color due to the depth of the atmosphere the sun's light has to penetrate before reaching the earth. But this shift is small, up to 500K depending where you live, which is a difference that's barely perceptible to the human eye.

On the other hand, daylight color definitely shifts across the duration of a single day. Sunlight starts out in the morning at approximately 2000K (red/orange), climbs above 5000K (white) at midday, then drops back to 2000K or lower at sunset. Daylight-sky color temp can climb as high as 8,000-10,000K (blue) on a sunny summer afternoon.

How did this myth come to be? It's likely the downstream effect of how HID lights found their way into indoor gardens. Initially, indoor gardeners used MH lamps to light their gardens. Then HPS lamps with a greater amount of red spectrum were introduced to indoor gardening, and the gardeners who tried them found that these new lights significantly improved the weight of their harvests.

Someone postulated that MH spectrum was better for vegetative growth and HPS spectrum better for flowering, and the myth was born. Unfortunately "blue light for vegging" and "red light for flowering" still persists today although the industry is finally beginning to move past it.

Just after LED grow lights were introduced, some manufacturers took this to the extreme and were pitching *only* blue light for vegetative growth and *only* red light for flowering. Be aware as of 2019 there are *still* manufacturers preaching this false concept and manufacturing lights that can be red or blue only but they are quickly disappearing. Red or blue only *might* work for low-light crops, but the light-loving plants we typically grow indoors need a more complete spectrum to grow properly. Don't fall for it.

90 LED Watts Can Replace 400-600 HID Watts

MYTH Oh, how most of you missed out on the "fun" of the early days of LED grow lights! When LED grow lights were first introduced, one manufacturer boldly proclaimed that their single 90 watt LED grow light would outperform a 400 or 600 watt HID. These claims were laughable then, and they're still laughable now. Early LED grow light manufacturers were hugely overzealous with their claims, which they "proved" by growing wheatgrass or lettuce instead of light-hungry crops such as tomatoes or cannabis.

Testing revealed that these early "90 watt" units actually drew only 54-56 watts of power at the wall, on average. With a few of those watts powering onboard cooling fans, these lights actually produced less usable light than 75-100 watts of HID–not anywhere near the 400 or 600 watt HID performance claimed by their manufacturers.

At least the industry is beginning to learn its lesson. Although still rare at the completion of this edition, some LED grow light manufacturers provide realistic power ratings and coverage area recommendations for their lights. This combined with better, more efficient LEDs and more effective lighting designs are helping to end this myth. It would be ideal for LED grow light manufacturers to publish tables showing the output of their lights in PPFD at set height intervals so that we, their customers, can decide for ourselves how much HID these lights replace in the actual conditions we face in our gardens.

Emitter Power Equals Penetration Potential

MYTH The claim by some early LED grow lights manufacturers that higher wattage emitters penetrated deeper into the canopy is just plain silly. Plants are very good at grabbing up PAR photons, which are immediately absorbed on exposure (except for some of the green ones). The leaves at the top will absorb nearly all the PAR photons before they have a chance to penetrate deeper into the canopy. Better penetration comes from physically manipulating the plant such as removing selected leaves and branches so light can shine deeper into the plant or making the light more diffuse so photons of lower angles can penetrate between the top leaves and get absorbed by the next set of leaves… not from emitter wattage.

For the commercial cannabis grower, deep canopy penetration comes not from the grow light directly over a plant, it comes from the lights next to the one above. Having a wide beam angle is key as narrow beam angles won't supply any light to adjacent plants. Since cannabis grows kind of like a Christmas tree with distinct levels, the "light next door" can penetrate between the levels, exposing photons to the inner leaves.

LEDs Produce No Heat

MYTH One of the most-misused sales pitch for LED grow lights is that they produce little to no heat. When a manufacturer makes this claim about their LED grow light, it makes me wonder whether the manufacturer has ever used one for anything more than a photo shoot. Sure, LED grow lights produce *less* heat than HID grow lights, but there is still heat, and that heat needs to be managed. See for yourself: garden temperature will drop immediately after an LED grow light switches off, just like in an HID garden. Besides we now know there is 3.412 BTU released for every watt used in our grow facilities. No heat–no way!

White Light for You

If you're a commercial grower that has taken my advice and is not growing under a burple light, you can skip to the next section. This information is for the hobby crowd who may consider using a burple light if it fits their needs.

Some LED grow lights include white emitters, this might be enough for the task of examining your garden. If your LED grow light does not include white emitters, or not enough to see clearly, hang a small fluorescent light or two in the garden to help you see what you're missing. It's just more light to your plants, but a possible garden-saver for you. Don't get lazy and skip this part–this is experience talking.

Plug the fluorescent light(s) into a plug strip, extension cord, or socket that is controlled by your LED grow light timer and *not* directly into a wall socket, so it can't accidently be left on and interrupt the dark cycle. Anytime you suspect a problem, and not less than once a week, turn the burple LED grow light(s) off during the light cycle, and give your garden a careful inspection with just the white light on. Don't forget to turn the LED grow light back on after you're done.

5. LED Grow Lights: The Fixture

The last chapter dug into the details about the light that LED grow lights produce. This chapter explores the light fixtures themselves, from the emitters inward, including what to look for in an LED grow light manufacturer. This information should arm you to select and purchase the best LED grow light for your requirements.

What is an LED?

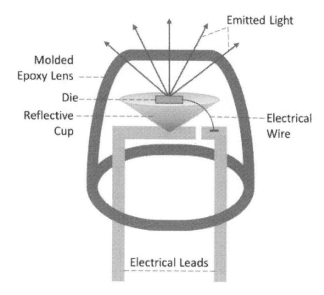

LED is an acronym for light emitting diode. LEDs differ from HID lamps in that they use a semiconductor diode to produce light instead of a hot, glowing gas plasma. When an electric current is passed through an LED, a tiny chunk of material at the center of the emitter called a "die" glows a particular color depending on the material it's made from. The die sits in a reflective cup to direct the light outward through an affixed epoxy lens, and then the entire thing is enclosed in an epoxy case.

A grow light made with LEDs consists of the emitters, a heat sink, a driver(s), optional cooling fans, and a housing to enclose it all. Individual emitters are connected to a circuit board that's bonded to a heat sink, which along with any cooling fans disperses the heat the LEDs generate. The light's driver, analogous to a ballast in HID lighting, provides power to the emitters.

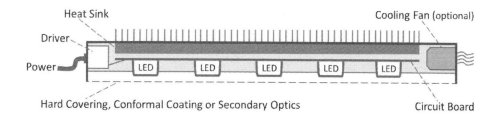

LED BIN Codes

When it comes to LEDs, the term **BIN** is an acronym for **brightness index number**. It's a multi-digit number that indicates the LED's brightness and color rating. Many people are confused about this term, thinking that BIN means a physical sorting bin instead of an abbreviation. They may believe that a "higher BIN" is physically above a "lower BIN" on a shelf or rack.

Unfortunately, not all LEDs emitters are created equal. Wide quality variances arise during the LED manufacturing process, partly because of raw material quality differences. The LED manufacturing process ends with testing the output of each batch, which is measured and sold by its BIN rating.

This testing requirement is one of the scale problems facing LED manufacturers: it's expensive and time consuming to test each batch, but current manufacturing processes and raw material quality don't leave them any choice. The testing process results in emitters being separated into different quality classes and assigned BIN codes that describe efficacies and peak wavelengths / kelvin ratings. The cost of the emitter is based on the BIN code.

Ceramic vs. Plastic-Packaged LEDs

The horticultural lighting industry has a dirty little secret that I'm going to expose. Until recently, most of the white LED emitters used in LED grow lights were made with cheap plastic packaging. This type of packaging has a significantly shorter lifespan than ceramic packaging.

Plastic-packaged LEDs will typically cross the L90 threshold after only 6,000 hours or approximately 1.4 years of typical use with a surface temperature of 185°F/85°C. The early degradation of plastic-packaged LEDs is why many early commercial adopters of LED grow lights had great success for the first year then began to regret their purchase over the following years.

With plastic-based LEDs, L70 is typically crossed after only 16,700 hours or approximately 3.8 years. This is nowhere near the routinely touted 50,000 expected hours of use. As of this edition, I still see plastic emitters quite often in hobby grade LED grow lights but they are increasingly less common in commercial units. Buyer beware.

The reason why plastic-packaged LEDs degrade early is the breaking down of their phosphor coatings. White LEDs start their lives as blue emitters. Through the use of a phosphor coating, the color is expanded into the green, yellow, orange and red regions resulting in an overall white "color" such as 2700K or 6500K.

The phosphor coating on plastic LEDs begins to crack over time. This shortens the length of the pathway within the phosphor that the photon travels through before being emitted. The longer a photon travels through the phosphor, the more it "slows down", thus lowering its energy level. Shortening this pathway shifts the light output towards the blue region (higher Kelvin ratings). Additionally, photon density drops as the cracking continues.

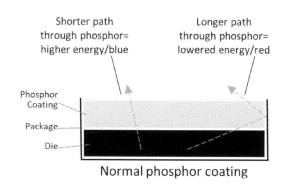

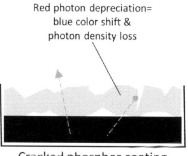

Normal phosphor coating   Cracked phosphor coating

Chip on Board

Chip on Board LEDs are relatively new. Commonly called "**COBs**" they consist of multiple emitters, typically nine or more, affixed directly to a substrate to form a single light module. When energized, they look like a lighted panel than multiple individual light sources. Lots of light can be generated in a small space with this technology. COBs typically consume 3-90 watts. LED chip manufacturers are currently producing COB packages that achieve high photon efficacies.

Are COBs useful in LED grow lights? They do put out a lot of photons and several LED grow light manufacturers currently selling LED grow lights that utilize COB technology. The major problem is light density—COBs put out a bunch of light in a small space, almost like a flashlight. It would be a challenge to get good light uniformity over a large indoor grow with COB LEDs. Thus, COBs have yet to find a home in commercial indoor grow operations and it's unlikely that they will. For hobby grade lights, maybe.

COBs may find a home in another type of fixture—one that is designed for greenhouse operations. In a greenhouse, the last thing you want to do is block sunlight with your lights (or anything else for that matter). With their small physical size and dense light output, COBs could be great for supplemental lighting in a greenhouse. This is yet another area where more research is required.

LEDs: Mid vs. High-Power

LEDs are also categorized by the amount of electricity they consume. In addition to COBs, LEDs are classified as medium and high power. **Medium power LEDs** typically draw 0.2-1.0 watts. They work best when paired with secondary optics, with multiple emitters sharing a single focal lens (more on secondary optics later in this chapter). **High power LEDs** usually fall into the 1.0-5.0 watt range. They may and may not include secondary optics. LED grow light manufacturers have to balance the performance of each type when designing a light. Good news for the average grower is who cares? Its only about PPFD!

Beam Angle

LED emitters all include an internal lens that controls the direction of the light that's emitted. These internal lenses are generally described by the angle of the light that streams out of the emitter, measured in degrees, known as the "beam angle".

The smaller the beam angle, the more directly the light is focused downward. So-called "narrow" beam angles are typically less than 60 degrees. A narrow beam angle causes the area directly beneath the LED grow light to be strongly illuminated, but the light will not spread outside of the grow light's actual physical size. Larger beam angles spread the light out more, providing less intense light directly beneath the LED grow light but with a spread that can exceed the grow light's size. Wide beam lens angles are 60 to 150 degrees.

There are two different methods for measuring beam angles. The first and less common method looks for the angle at which 10% of the peak intensity is reached on each side of the origin (the center). The more common method looks for the angle that has 50% of the peak intensity is reached on either side of the origin. This method is called "Full-Width, Half-Max" (FWHM). For example, if a LED is measured to have 50% of its intensity at 45°, its beam angle would be 90°.

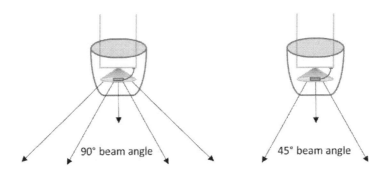

Remote Phosphor

Remote phosphor is a newer technology designed to create white light from LEDs. A royal-blue LED die is used as the initial source. Its light is transmitted through a mixing chamber before it strikes a remote phosphor coating on the inside of the LED grow light lens/globe. The characteristics of the remote phosphor coating will determine the light wavelengths emitted by the lamp.

Remote phosphor LED lights are making their debut in human lighting. They do a great job of smoothing out the light produced without secondary optics. Remote phosphor's main advantage over traditional white LEDs is that they provide highly uniform light output.

Another advantage to remote phosphor technology is we don't have to be as picky about LED BIN selection. If an LED light was made with traditional white LEDs, and even one emitter had a different BIN than the others, light from that lamp could look funky to the human eye. The mixing chamber in a remote phosphor lamp evens out the light from its various emitters prior to that light striking the phosphor costing, thus reducing or eliminating issues related to varying BIN ratings amongst similar LED emitters.

Industry experts don't agree whether remote phosphor technology will find its place in grow facilities. We'll have to see how effective remote phosphor LED grow lights are at producing PAR light. At the time this book was published there was at least one LED grow light manufacturer offering a grow light using remote phosphor technology. It's a smaller light that could work in a hobby garden but not commercial settings.

3watt/3 Explained

This section on this type of LED emitters is one place where my material is a bit dated. I am not aware of anyone still using these emitters in newly manufactured LED commercial grow lights... but I could be wrong! I have left this section just in case you run across a grow light with so-called "3watt/3" type emitters, though I have deleted information that has since been proven incorrect.

When considering LED grow lights that claim to include 2 or 3 watt LEDs, make sure you understand what you're actually getting. If the LED emitters in the light are labeled "2watt/2" or "3watt/3," this means that two or three 1 watt emitters have been placed under a single lens and are being <u>called</u> higher wattage emitters. This is misleading. Three emitters under a single lens typically generate more heat than a true 3 watt emitter, thus limiting the current the combined emitter can handle, which in turn lowers the amount of light the "3watt/3" LED produces to something less than a true 3 watt emitter.

How Many Emitters Does It Take?

One of the more common "technical" questions I receive about a particular LED grow light is how many emitters does it have? This question is one of those "red flag" warnings that the person who is asking needs to understand what's important–PPFD–not what it takes to get to those levels. How many emitters, the forwarding voltage(s), etc. are *very* important to the designers of the light but not relevant to the end user– PPFD is.

The same goes for the LED grow light manufacturers. Far too often I see the number of emitters and currents at which they operate described in LED grow light marketing materials. When I talk to these manufacturers it becomes apparent very quickly that they have no clue what they are talking about. If you see this, even in hobby grade lights, walk away. They are "me-too" players and probably won't be around in the future for support.

The blame for this bragging-about-our-parts problem may lie with the LED emitter manufacturers. Some of them have "advertising co-op" programs that will contribute to their customers' marketing budgets if they mention the manufacturer's name in their marketing materials and/or packaging.

Golden Sample

Unscrupulous LED light manufacturers have been known to produce demonstration units with high-quality emitters and then switch to cheaper emitters for their production products. The term given to this bait-and-switch is "golden sample".

While there's really no way to know without an integrating sphere whether the grow light you're buying was made with high- or low-quality emitters, you can protect yourself by buying only from reputable LED grow light manufacturers and suppliers.

Heat Sinks

Creating light also creates heat, even for chemical light sources such as glow sticks and the oceanic dinoflagellates that cause red tides. No lighting source 100% efficient. And so, like all electrically driven light sources, LEDs used in grow lights require cooling. High operating temperatures cause LED lights to emit fewer photons and can dramatically reduce the lifespan of the lights. Overheated LEDs can also shift their output wavelength so that the light no longer delivers the advertised spectrum. Since we specifically chose the wavelengths we wanted our plants to receive when we bought our LED grow lights, it would be silly to screw it all up by not removing the light's heat properly.

The best way to cool LED grow lights is with a heat sink: a metal block inside the grow light that absorbs then radiates the light's heat into the surrounding air. Calculating the exact size required is a job for the professionals. It's dependent on the target operating temperature of the fixture and many other factors.

To save costs, some LED grow lights feature undersized heat sinks. Remaining excess heat is removed by blowing air from a small cooling fan across the heat sink. This design produces "false savings": not only is the heat sink inadequately sized to remove enough heat, the fan introduces an unnecessary failure point. A failed fan on a light with an inadequate heat sink will cause the light to overheat, reducing performance and possibly damaging the light. Always select an LED grow light with a big enough heat sink and don't rely on a fan to save the day.

This can get worse—some LED grow lights that utilize fans for cooling blow air directly across sensitive electronic parts within the LED fixture. This can blow dirt, water and chemicals into the electronics leading to failures. If you can see any electronics through the fan you should probably skip on purchasing that light.

Water Cooling

Just about every indoor gardening light source has been water cooled at one point or another and LEDs are no exception. Personally, I am not a fan of water-cooled lights as the thought of purposely placing water next to or inside electronics can be a recipe for disaster. One of the major selling points of LEDs is that they produce less heat, so what is the need for water-cooled LED grow lights?

Water cooling adds an extreme level of complexity to the build and operation of a grow facility. Since another selling point of LEDs is simpler installation and operation, why make these things more difficult? You would need to run a massive amount of water lines in a large facility to support water-cooled lights. Then you need to remove the heat from the water which requires a water chiller. And, of course, you'll need one or more pumps to keep it all under pressure while you wait for leaks.

There is another problem with using water cooled lights. Condensation a natural byproduct of transferring chilled water lines. This dripping water must also be dealt with, adding yet another layer of complexity.

There might technically be savings from water-cooled grow lights, as water chilling is typically more efficient than air-conditioning. But are these real-world savings? Setting aside the cost to build and maintain an elaborate system of water lines, pump(s), reservoir(s) and chiller(s), ask yourself how many people are trained in air-conditioning vs. water chillers. If your A/C failed you could get it fixed fairly quickly, with a water chiller maybe not.

One application where water cooling has a place is in research. If an experimental protocol called for exact temperature management, water cooled LEDs could be the solution. Systems could be designed to recirculate the light's heat in clever ways such as placing heat exchangers where heat is needed. This could allow for total thermodynamic control of experiments (on a small scale).

Drivers

LED grow lights don't have ballasts like HID lights. Instead, they use **drivers** (aka "power supplies") to deliver the correct voltage and current (amperage) to the LEDs. Physically, a driver can be a simple resistor or a complicated, constant current driver made up of numerous electronic components. LED grow lights may have multiple drivers to separately control various colors or banks of emitters within the light.

Resistor-based drivers are inexpensive components that produce a fixed voltage and current. These components are sensitive to temperature change, so with a resistor-based driver, as the internal temperature of the grow light increases, the light output will decrease. These drivers should not be used in LED grow lights.

Constant Current drivers produce a constant current level regardless of the surrounding temperature. They have sensing circuits that allow the driver to accommodate the effect of temperature changes and regulate the current accordingly. They are found in modern LED grow lights.

Constant Voltage drivers produce fixed output voltage of 12 or 24 volts. They have an advantage when the LED design calls for multiple strings of LEDs wired in parallel. This overcomes the problem of attempting to balance the current across all the strings. They are found less often in today's LED grow lights.

Constant Current / Constant Voltage drivers combine both technologies. The driver initially powers up in constant voltage mode. It stays in this mode until the draw exceeds the set current upper limit. Once this set point is crossed, the drive switches to constant current mode. This type of driver is also found in current LED grow lights.

Protecting the Emitters

LED emitters are sensitive electronic components and need protection. They can come loose or get damaged if physically struck. Even the simple process of cleaning the light can dislodge an emitter that's not protected by a physical barrier such as secondary optics or a hard covering over the LEDs.

Conformal Coatings

The least expensive way to protect LEDs is to apply a conformal coating, which is a thin (25-75 μm) polymeric film which 'conforms' to the contours of a printed circuit board offering some protection from dust, moisture and chemicals. The thickness of the coating can shift the color output so proper design is required. Conformal coatings have an advantage as they block less of the photons than other types of protection.

The downside of conformal coatings is that they offer limited protection for the emitters. Relying on the coating in a commercial operation might be risky. Commercial grows typically conduct lots of spraying as part of integrated pest management programs. No matter how careful growers are while spraying, grow lights still at least occasionally get sprayed. That creates lots of delicate lights to clean, which is problematic because conformal coatings can be rubbed off, which can create a really bad situation in which the emitters themselves might get exposed to sprays.

Another problem is conformal coatings offer no protection from the emitter being physically dislodged when cleaned or hit. A mop or broom handle could destroy a light that is only protected by a conformal coating. Grow lights with conformal coatings definitely have their place in hobby gardens since less light is being blocked. Just take extreme care when cleaning, spraying or working in the garden.

Hard Coverings

Commercial grade fixtures need better protection for the emitters than a simple coating. There are three common choices–glass, acrylic and polycarbonate. All three are used in LED grow lights. While all of these cover materials pass roughly 90% of the light through, differences in weight, durability and price may make one cover material better than the others for a specific grow operation.

I learned the need for hard coverings firsthand an employee of mine smacked a mop handle into a fixture that was protected by a conformal coating. It was a hard hit. To my surprise it didn't fail or so I thought. When I arrived the next morning, the light didn't turn on. I learned... protect your emitters in commercial grow facilities.

The following chart compares the strengths and weaknesses of these different grow light cover materials:

	Glass	Acrylic (Plexiglas)	Polycarbonate (Lexan)
Light Transmission	90%	92%	88%
Scratch Resistance	High	Medium	Low
Impact Resistance	Low	Medium	High
UV Transmission	Yes	Yes	Yes
Yellows	No	No	Yes
Expense	$	$$	$$$
Weight	Heavy	Light	Light
Flexibility	Rigid	Rigid	Flexible

Secondary Optics

I've changed my mind again about secondary optics. Secondary optics are small lenses applied on top of the emitters that focus the photons produced by the emitter onto your garden. They can focus the light of a single emitter or several under the same lens. What's the point in generating lots of photons if they light up the walls? If you want that result, get an HID!

Any LED grow light that is going to be used in a commercial grow facility NEEDs some hard covering over the LEDs. If you're going to block some of the transmitted light why not take advantage and focus it at the same time?

You can recognize LED grow lights with secondary optics because their light panel doesn't look like a bunch of emitters stuck into a sheet of metal. Secondary lenses are made from optical plastic and come in many shapes and sizes depending on the desired light distribution.

When 200 Watts Is 300 Watts

This section is for the hobby growers. You commercial guys can skip ahead. As if it was not complicated enough to choose an LED grow light, LED manufacturers use different specifications to describe their lights. The power level of LED grow lights maybe described as the amount of "wall watts" consumed (energy drawn from an electrical outlet), the number of LEDs in the light multiplied by their maximum allowable power, or some other totally made up number.

For example, an LED grow light with 100 3 watt emitters that uses 200 wall watts could be advertised as either a 200 or 300 watt LED grow light. Wall watts are what counts when measuring LED grow light power consumption—or at least the most important when it comes to not overloading an electric circuit.

Why does this matter? To your garden, it doesn't. Your garden doesn't care what yardstick the manufacturer uses in a marketing pitch. However, it does matter when determining actual fixture performance when comparing different LED grow lights, that is (here we go again), how much PPFD they produce.

IP Ratings

Grow rooms are inherently wet and dirty places. Not only are watering/irrigating and spraying common grow room activities, grow rooms are often completely washed down between each harvest. While I don't think anyone is intentionally going to high pressure wash their lights, grow lights do need protection from water.

 **EXPERT CORNER**

Underwriters Lab (UL) "wet-rating" is approximately equivalent to IP65.

The IP Code system classifies and rates the degree of protection provided against dust and water/chemicals intrusion of an individual component or the entire fixture. These ratings provide a much better description beyond just "waterproof" or "water resistant". IP ratings describe the level of protection in two digits. The first digit has a range of 0-6 and describes how well the device is protected from solid particle penetration. The second digit has a range of 0-8 and defines the liquid penetration protection level.

Ingress Protection Level			
Solids		**Liquids**	
1	>50 mm	1	Vertical water drops
2	>12.5 mm	2	15° angle water drops
3	>2.5 mm	3	60° angle water spray
4	>1 mm	4	Water splash in all directions
5	Mostly dust tight	5	Water jets
6	Dust tight	6	Powerful water jets
		7	1 meter submersion for 30 min
		8	Submersion under pressure for long periods

From the chart, a fixture that has an IP67 rating is completely impervious to dust and can tolerate being submerged to a depth of 1 meter for 30 minutes.

Wireless Controllers

Several LED grow light manufacturers have come out with wireless controllers for their lights. These systems offer effortless control over the lights with features including simulated sunrise/sunset, spectrum change, and dimming in addition to routine light/dark cycle scheduling. While I will discuss the issues associated with these changes in light levels in the next chapter, there is something else very concerning about wireless controls.

A few years ago, I asked just about every grow light manufacturer that offers wireless controls about the security protocols they use to protect the wireless connection from being intruded or read. They all have the same response–a blank stare. Without adequate security, it would not be that difficult to "hack in" and take control of the lights. All you need to do is determine which type of network is being used (there are several to choose from), buy one of the controller modules, stand or park nearby, and intercept the signal.

It seems that grow light manufacturers never considered why anyone would want to "hack" a grow light. But what's to stop a competitor who learns you have an open connection to your lights (from a disgruntled employee, perhaps?) from doing mischievous things such as interrupting the dark cycle. For some plants, even a 5- to 10-minute light exposure during the dark cycle could disrupt their transition between vegetative and flowering states.

In the last edition I stated that commercial growers should stay away for wireless controllers because of the lack of security. Flash forward to the end of 2019 and security has improved dramatically. Cannabis legalization has brought experts from other industries into the mix, bringing innovation with them particularly from the IoT arena. Wireless network security is becoming less of a concern.

One thing it to consider is facility size when deploying wireless controllers. Some of the current wireless protocols are very "dirty" and emit excessive EMF radiation that can disrupt other electronic and communication at the facility. Large facility operators should look for wireless solutions use wireless protocols designed for use with lighting that produce less overhead digital noise. There are several companies deploying this type of wireless technology at the writing of this book.

LED Grow Light Designs

LED grow lights come in five basic designs: a large surface covered with emitters, light heads with multiple emitters under the same lens, lights with clusters or "rosettes" of emitters, intra-canopy lights and tube lights that resemble fluorescent lamps, some of which can be used in regular fluorescent light fixtures.

Large Surface LED Grow Lights

The first large surface LED grow lights to come to market looked like someone loaded up a shotgun and blasted LED emitters across a flat metal sheet. Some LED grow lights feature densely packed emitters across the entire downward surface of the grow light while others space them out. These lights may or may not include secondary optics.

Large surface LED grow lights for the hobby market have not changed too much since the last edition. Newer ones feature higher power LEDs in the 3 to 5 watts per emitter range, some with COBs in the 50+ watt range, which the LED grow light manufacturers market heavily as penetrating more deeply into the canopy (perpetuating the emitter power equals penetration potential myth).

Commercial LED grow lights have changed quite a bit since the first edition, in fact, this segment barely existed then. Instead of using dozens of high power emitters in a grow light, LED manufacturers targeting commercial grows are using hundreds to thousands of LED emitters, surface mounted close together, under secondary optics, running at lower current levels. Lowering the current level of an LED can improve its lighting efficacy. These lights spread their emitters over greater area often closely mimicking the actual size of the targeted grow area. Some are quite large and this design concept is delivering on its promise of better light uniformity and distribution.

- Advantages: Square- or rectangular-shaped grow lights provide even illumination that conforms to the shape of many indoor gardens
- Disadvantages: Can be heavy and bulky
- What to look for: Large heat sink to dissipate the heat concentrated by many LEDs

Clusters/Rosettes

LEDs arranged in clusters was among the second generation of LED grow light designs to hit the market and for the most part have disappeared. In these lights, lots of LEDs are closely packed together, with spaces between the clusters. Think of them as portholes on a ship, where the emitter groups are the holes and they are evenly spaced down the length of the light. Some manufacturers mount their clusters inside a metal box while others mount them on bars, with multiple bars typically used to customize light coverage for the garden.

- Advantages: On some units, if one cluster fails it can be removed and replaced by the end user
- Disadvantages: Not all lights that employ clusters are end-user replaceable
- What to look for: End-user replaceable clusters. Even cluster spacing for optimum coverage. Correct beam angles and distribution of rosettes to match garden shape.

Tube-Style LED Bars

Tube style LED lights are long tubes similar to a fluorescent lamp but filled with LEDs. Most are approximately the size of a T8 fluorescent lamp. They come equipped with internal voltage regulation, so there is no need for an external driver. Be sure to use only the fluorescent lighting fixtures recommended by the LED tube light manufacturer–standard fluorescent fixtures with an internal ballast can destroy the LED tube. If the LED tube manufacturer doesn't specify a particular lighting fixture, then use fixtures that are directly wired, with the ballast removed. If you are unfamiliar with this type of work, consult an electrician.

- Advantages: Square or rectangular shape of tube-style grow light fixtures mimics the size and shape of many indoor gardens. If one tube fails, the others are unaffected. Some light fixtures on the market combine LED and fluorescent grow light tubes, which can enhance performance over fluorescent grow lights used alone. Some can be directly replaced into existing fluorescent fixtures without removal of the existing ballast.
- Disadvantages: Low PPFD. Best deployed for growing low light intensity crops
- What to look for: Tubes that provide proper spectra and PPFD for the garden

Intra-Canopy LEDs

Intra-canopy garden lights place LED emitters within the plant canopy in addition to above it. The lights can be chained together offering a flexible solution that is usually deployed in small rigid channels. There are few intra-canopy garden lighting solutions currently on the market, and this lighting method has not gained much popularity to date.

Though intra-canopy maybe helpful in delivering more PAR to the plant canopy, they tend to illuminate the undersides of cannabis leaves. This is not the most effective orientation as chlorophylls are concentrated on the top of the leaf. I personally have only seen intra-canopy lighting used as supplemental lighting in greenhouses growing tomatoes. If you think about the twisted leaf structures of tomatoes vs. the structured levels of a cannabis plant, intra-canopy makes sense for lighting tomatoes but not cannabis. Maybe someone will prove me wrong.

- Advantages: Won't block overhead lighting. Can help increase DLI
- Disadvantages: Unproven effectiveness–possibly crop specific
- What to look for: Durability and IP65 minimum rating

"Chainable" Lights

Many smaller hobby grade LED grow lights can be chained together so that several lights can share one electrical wall outlet. If an LED grow light is chainable, the manufacturer will specify how many can be chained together. Never exceed the recommended number of chained lights, or you risk overloading the circuitry. When chaining grow lights together, use zip ties or straps to keep the cords between lights out of the way.

- Advantages: Simplifies grow room setup and allows you to use one timer to turn all the lights on or off at the same time
- Disadvantages: If one light fails, it might bring the whole chain down with it. This varies between lights, depending on how they are wired. For this reason, some growers prefer to plug multiple lights into a plug strip then plug the strip into a single timer.
- What to look for: Lights with secure cord connectors that will not dislodge easily. UL listing for these lights is mandatory and difficult to find due to associated costs for proper design.

Indoor vs. Greenhouse Fixtures

There is quite a difference in physical design between a LED grow light heading for an indoor grow or to a greenhouse. Indoors the light is the primary source. It can be any size or shape as long as it delivers photons to the plants. There's no natural sunlight indoor to block. Commercial indoor lights should not use fans to cool them. Heat sinks can be made to the proper size to passively convection heat.

On the other hand, greenhouse supplementation lights must conform to specific physical design requirements. The fixture must be physically small so as to not block natural sunlight. Fans can be used in greenhouse lights if done properly. The main challenge to the LED grow light manufacturer that wants to produce greenhouse lights is they don't know how the fixture will be deployed. Greenhouse lights deployed in a tall greenhouse with the fixture bolted at gutter level can get significantly hotter than those hung close to the canopy.

Cooling fans should be designed as backups, not as the main cooling method-heat sinks are still mandatory. They should be connected to a thermocouple (heat sensor) and turned on when needed on hot days. Multiple fans should be used, with one fan having plenty of power to cool the fixture on the hottest of days in case one fails. Additionally, greenhouse lights with fans should have a thermocouple should have the ability to turn the light down or off in the rare event of both fans failing.

Like everything, fan technology has moved considerably forward. It's now possible to find 100,000 hour rated, IP68 fans that are perfect for cooling greenhouse fixtures. They will withstand the potentially dirty greenhouse environment and can be pressure washed and even submerged.

Types of LED Grow Light Suppliers

LED grow lights are a sizeable investment so do your homework before buying one, or one hundred. Try to learn as much about the manufacturer as you can before making this investment. Take the time to email questions to manufacturers whose lights you are considering including questions listed in the "Purchasing an LED Grow Light" section.

Sloper Says

When discussing a particular light with its manufacturer make sure all the performance metrics add up. If they don't or are outrageous claims MOVE ON!!

Also ask the questions from the next section regarding warranty service. See how complete their answers are and how long it takes for their response. Alternatively give them a call and discuss the light you're considering. The better manufacturers will have a customer support line.

LED grow light manufacturers fall into five basic types:

Research and Development Company

I'm happy to say there is a new type of LED grow light manufacturer to add to the list. There are a few manufacturers that are moving the industry forward that I classify as "research and development" LED grow light companies. These manufacturers are designing, testing and field prototyping their own lights not just repurposing an existing architectural light with an altered spectrum for plant growth.

R&D grow light companies don't typically rely on data from the LED emitter manufacturers. They have their own integrating spheres and do their own testing. These LED grow light manufacturers are the ones to seek out when purchasing lights for a commercial grow operation.

Large, Well-Funded Company

Well-funded companies that produce or distribute LED grow lights on a large scale are becoming more common. They usually have strong relationships with their vendors and so have access to top-quality components. These grow light suppliers can quickly send out a replacement or loaner light if there's a problem.

They are likely to have support staff available to take phone calls and can ship in a timely manner. On the other hand, well-established LED grow light suppliers may not be able to adapt to change as quickly as smaller companies. They may need to burn through existing stock before making changes to their lights. These manufacturers may be producing lights for both the hobby and commercial markets. Far too often these companies are simply repurposing fixtures that were designed with some other application in mind.

Small Manufacturer

When this book was originally written, most LED grow light suppliers were small, often underfunded companies. These early-stage companies build or import small lots of grow lights without much in the way of inventory reserves or spares. They tend to deliver slowly—you may end up waiting for them to receive critical components before they can build your light.

Some of these manufacturers produce top-quality lights and have the support to back them up, but some don't. Use your gut when considering one of their lights. Will they be in business long enough to support their warranty? Can they deliver to your expectations? If you can live with some uncertainty but feel good about a small manufacturer and their light, go for it. You may discover a great light at a great price. Small manufacturers tend to produce lights for the hobby market.

Drop Ship Direct

Companies that drop ship direct from overseas LED grow light manufacturers, instead of maintaining their own inventory, are generally "me too" players trying to ride the LED wave and make a fast buck without putting a significant amount of their own capital at risk. These suppliers generally have limited technical expertise and may not be able to answer basic questions about indoor gardening or the lights they distribute. The two concerns in dealing with these companies are the quality of their products, particularly the emitters, and shipping timeliness.

Drop ship direct LED sellers also have limited customer service abilities—if your light breaks, you generally have to ship it back to where it was made (likely overseas, which is potentially expensive and slow), wait for a repair, and then wait again for the grow light to be shipped back. This can take several weeks—can your garden survive that long without light? Probably not.

Unfortunately, this type of supplier is becoming more common as the market continues to expand. If you can identify one, run away. Remember, there are a lot of very clever Internet sites that look great but are not the real deal. Drop ship direct merchants exclusively service the hobby market.

Homebuilt

Last is the classic "DIY" homebuilt LED grow light. Someone put lots of life energy into producing what they considered to be the perfect light. How good are these lights? That all depends on how they were built and with what components.

One of the best things about DIY grow lights is that they can often be changed as technology evolves— since you built it or know who did, you're in a great position to resolve issues and upgrade your light. If you're handy with a soldering iron so to speak, go for it—your LED grow light might be a game changer.

Purchasing an LED Grow Light

One way to judge an LED grow light manufacturer is by the information they provide on their specification sheets, website and other marketing materials. Do they have complete information? Are they making wild claims? Make sure to collect and analyze the information below when deciding about an LED grow light.

The most important things to verify:

- PPF (umol/s)
- Actual fixture wattage draw
- PAR photon efficacy (umol/J)
- Spectral Power Distribution (SPD) chart / light spectra
- Third party photometric lab results
- Example lighting layout for a "typical" grow room with average PPFD
- Safety certification (UL or other)
- IP55 grade minimum for commercial applications

Things that are irrelevant:

- LED emitter manufacturer
- Voltage and current at which the LEDs operate
- "LED wattage" = sum of the max wattage ratings of the LEDs x # of LEDs

Things that are obvious red flags:

- Crop yield improvement claims–especially after a single trial
- Claims of magical spectra or certain spectrum being critical for certain growth phases
- When the data doesn't add up, for example, a single PPFD measurements directly under the fixture divided by the light's wattage which results in impossible photon efficacy numbers

My Light Failed–Now What?

This next section is primarily for the hobbyists. Commercial growers should work with their lighting manufacturer, as well as the manufacturers of everything else in the grow operation, to develop a plan for when things inevitably fail.

Any type of grow light can fail; what happens should your grow light fail is one of the most of the overlooked buying criteria. Overcoming a failed grow light is more difficult in LED-based gardens than HID gardens since it's cost prohibitive to keep a spare LED light sitting around "just in case". Switching back to an HID light mid-grow presents all sorts of problems, since you use different gardening techniques with LED grow lights.

For any grow light you're considering, ask the manufacturer the questions listed below in order to "vet" their ability to help you should the light fail. Make sure you're talking to the actual manufacturer instead of a distributor such as a retail or online hydroponic equipment shop. While these distributors may be the only places where you can buy an LED grow light, they can only convey warranty information provided to them by the light's manufacturer—which may not include the answers you need.

When you're getting serious about buying an LED grow light, make sure you get straight and believable answers to these questions:

- Where was the light made? Where is it repaired?
- Will the manufacturer send a loaner? Does the manufacturer require a deposit for a loaner? How and when is the deposit refunded?
- Who pays for shipping, both to the repair facility and then back to you?
- Who owns manufacturing responsibilities, quality control, and customer support?
- Why do you think you will be in business in one, two, or three years in order to make good on your warranty?

6. Growing with LEDs

It takes a bit of experience to effectively grow with LED lights–just like it does when using any garden light. Why shouldn't it? If you're learning to garden indoors for the first time using LED grow lights, the advice in this book should be very helpful to get started, and with a little experience you should be off and running. If you're converting from HIDs, you'll need to make many changes to your gardening technique–most small but significant–to achieve the best yields possible.

Plant Types

The plant kingdom is very diverse. Scientists have come up with ways to group them based on growth characteristics. Understanding these major classifications will help you to know the recommended starting environmental conditions for the particular species you want to grow.

Short-Day vs. Day-Neutral vs. Long-Day Plants

One of the most important decisions to make about gardening indoors is how long to keep the lights on. This choice depends on what you're growing. The best photoperiod is different between types of plants and plant growth stages. Biologists have come up with a classification system based on plant photoperiod requirements: short-day, day-neutral, and long-day plants.

Don't let the names confuse you. Even though these categories are defined by how long the "day" is, it's really all about the dark. Scientists originally thought that day length was what triggered plants to fruit or flower, but now we know it's about phytochrome's conversion back to the P_r form during darkness that prompts it.

Short-day/long-night plants begin to form fruits or flowers as day length shortens and night length increases–sometime after summer solstice. These plants include fall-blooming flowers and fall-producing crops such as poinsettia, chrysanthemum, cotton, rice, and hemp.

Many plants don't care about day length and are therefore called "day neutral". These plants automatically fruit or flower when they get to a certain size or age, or when temperatures or humidity reach a certain range. Tulips, tomatoes, and many trees are day neutral.

Long-day/short-night plants initiate flowering when the nights begin to shorten. Many common vegetables and flowers are long-day plants such as lettuce, radish, spinach, potatoes, sunflowers, and daisies.

	Short-Day	Day-Neutral	Long-Day
When Plant Flowers or Fruits	When nights get longer (fall)	Independent of photoperiod	When nights get shorter (spring)
Example	Cotton, Rice, Cannabis	Roses, Tomatoes, Cucumbers	Spinach, Lettuce, Grasses
Flowering Photoperiod	12 hours or less	Independent	14-18 hours

What does this mean to you? For short-day plants, grow them up from seeds or cuttings with the lights on 18-20 hours a day, then change to a 12-hour-a-day light period to initiate flowering. For day-neutral plants, set the lights to run for 18 hours a day. For long-day plants, grow them up with 12 hours of light then change to 18-20 hours of light to flower. Give all plants uninterrupted darkness when the lights are off.

C_3, C_4, and CAM Plant Types

Plants are also classified by their method of acquiring CO_2 and the type of carbohydrates they create during photosynthesis. These groupings are called C_3, C_4, and CAM.

C_3 Photosynthesis

Ninety-five percent of all plants on the planet, including cannabis, are "C_3" plants. In addition to having woody stems and rounded leaves, these plants produce a compound that includes three carbon atoms as the product of photosynthesis–hence the name C_3. C_3 plants eat up supplemental CO_2 like candy, speeding up their photosynthetic process which makes more carbohydrates available for growth. C_3 plants open their stomata, small pores on the underside of their leaves, during the day to take CO_2 directly from the air. CO_2 supplementation is very effective for C_3 type plants.

C_4 Photosynthesis

"C_4" plants produce a post-photosynthesis molecule that contains four carbon atoms. They are mostly grasses including corn and other cereal grains. C_4 plants store CO_2 in an intermediate internal holding site thus concentrating it in the plant. Because of this, the C_4 photosynthetic process is a lot more efficient than the C_3 process–by up to six times in the right conditions.

C_4 plants keep their stomata closed and only open them when they need to refill their carbon stores. Thus, C_4 plants don't benefit very much from CO_2 supplementation because they have a built-in method to supplement carbon dioxide themselves.

CAM Photosynthesis

Plants that fall into the crassulacean acid metabolism (CAM) grouping are typically desert plants such as cacti and succulents. They open their stomata at night to collect CO_2 instead of during the day. Similar to C_4 plants, CAM plants make a four-carbon carbohydrates as their photosynthesis output. These plants are not typically grown indoors under electric lights.

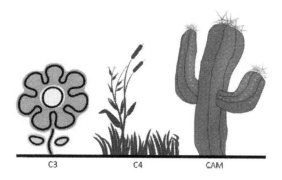

Genetics

Heavy harvests are mostly influenced by genetics. The best grower in the world with sub-par genetics is not going to win any awards. On the contrary, a rookie grower with great genetics could get lucky and hit it out of the park. This is the reason growers often maintain "mothers" (sometimes called a "donor" plant) to maintain their genetics.

Genotype and Phenotype

The **genotype** of a plant is the genetic code that contains all expressible (or potential) traits of a plant, also commonly called "variety" or "strain". A **phenotype** is a plant or plants that visibly express certain traits of their genotype, such as lanky or squatty physical shape. The phenotype depends upon the genotype but can also be influenced by environmental factors.

Phenotype expression is what makes growing from seed very unpredictable and therefore more of a challenge than growing from cuttings. Some seed varieties are very stable and predictable. This means you will get very similar plants year after year of planting them with little variation in phenotype expression. Stable genetics come from multiple back-crosses so the resultant offspring are very similar. Other seed varieties may not be as stable and thus their plants can be very different from seed to seed.

I prefer to grow from seed in my personal gardens, both indoors and out, because I like the variety of phenotype expression seeds bring. Seeds from the same genotype can typically be grown with the same nutritional regime and still have some uniqueness. When growing from clones, the only way to get a variance is to run different genotypes. This can be a challenge in a single grow due to differences in the physical size, shape, and nutritional demands between different genotypes.

> ### Sloper Says
> *Start more seeds than you need. Not all of them will make it and you can select the strongest ones from the survivors.*

Types of Seeds

There are many different types of seeds available. Some are good for breeding projects and others offer improved predictability.

Regular

"Regular" seeds are your typical mix of both male and female plants. They can be used as the basis of breeding projects. If you want to suppress seed formation in the offspring from these seeds, you may need to separate the males.

Feminized

Feminized seeds are female only and are another way of suppressing seed formation. They are typically created from female plants sprayed with hormones that stimulate seed production. Since the resulting feminized seeds come from female plants, there is no method to acquire male genetics.

F1, F2 etc.

A filial seed is the first offspring of two distinctly different parental types resulting in completely new genetic traits inherited from both parents–this is commonly associated with crossing two varieties. The number such as F1 or F2 refers to the number of times the line has been crossed. For example, if an F1 male and an F1 female plant produced seeds, those seeds would be F2.

S1

Self-pollinated or "selfing" seeds are spontaneously produced by the plant without outside genetics. These seeds tend to be very unstable and often result in plants that self-pollinate. You also may hear self-pollination resulting in seeds described as "herm'ing" which is short for hermaphrodite.

BX

Backcross seeds (BX) are the result of taking an offspring (filial) and breeding it back with a parent plant. This is typically done to stabilize and reinforce certain genetic traits. A seed can be the result of multiple generations of backcrossing. The multiple generations are labeled with a number such as BX1 or BX2.

IBL

Inbred line (IBL) seeds produce plants that are very similar in characteristics. These are stable genetics and are great for use in breeding projects. IBL seeds usually come from remote places where they have been isolated a very long time. These seeds are commonly referred to as "land-race".

Stages of Plant Growth

There are three basic stages of a plant's life: a seedling or clone, vegetative growth, and the fruiting/flowering stage. As summarized in the table later in this chapter, during each stage of their life, plants need different environmental conditions. This for the rest of this chapter it will be assumed that you're growing cannabis.

Cloning/Seed Starting with LEDs

Clones and starting seeds have very similar environmental needs. Growing from seed is just like it sounds–put a seed into a grow media of choice and feed/water it as necessary. Cloning is the process of taking a shoot from a donor plant and rooting it. Clones are copies of the donor plants, so start with the strongest, healthiest donor plants for a crop of vigorous cuttings.

 **Sloper Says**

Leave your clones alone once you have taken them. Many people like to handle them, move them, and pick them up, but it's not helpful. Keep them moist and leave them alone until fully rooted.

Also, since some plant species can produce plants that are either male or female, cloning allows the gardener to select for female-only gardens which is helpful when producing flowers and fruit, without having to sort through seedlings to pick only female sprouts. Using clones is also generally faster than growing from seed.

LED grow lights are fantastic for seedlings or clones. Their compact size and ease of use can turn almost any space into a seedling/clone garden. Even when LED grow lights were first introduced, it was clear that LEDs produced strong, bushy roots on clones and strong seed starts. Early studies indicate that a higher blue-to-red ratio causes cuttings to root faster than with other lights. This is an area that needs considerably more research.

Seedlings or clones don't need nearly as much light as plants in vegetative or flowering stages. In fact, too much light will stunt or kill them by pushing too much photosynthesis–the little seedlings and cuttings simply can't keep up. They rely on the stored carbohydrates in their stems and leaves, or in the seed itself, for the energy to produce roots–diverting this energy to defend against too much light will cause rooting to slow or stop, and the seedling or clone, to die.

Since clones don't have roots, they are susceptible to drying out. Many gardeners use humidity domes over their cutting trays to keep the moisture levels up. Humidity domes are critical for some plants but not for others so experiment to see what works best for your environment and plants.

If you're using a humidity dome, once your seedlings or cuttings have full, bushy roots, they are almost ready to move into their next stage: vegetative growth. But first they have to be "hardened off"–a process in which you slowly decrease the humidly under the dome. Clones accustomed to high humidity levels can dry out, wilt, and possibly die if the humidity is dropped to average room conditions too quickly. To harden off cuttings, lift the humidity dome and set it at an angle over the tray–carefully, so you don't crush the cuttings–for a couple of hours on the first day. This allows normal room air to penetrate the dome and gradually reduce the humidity.

Keep a close eye on your cuttings during hardening off–many gardeners rush the process and kill clones at this stage. Gradually increase this time for a few days adding an hour or two a day, then start leaving the humidity dome completely off for a few hours, gradually increasing this time until the cuttings are fully adjusted to normal room air conditions. At this point, the rooted cuttings are ready to move into the vegetative growth phase.

Cloning and seed-starting tips:

- Use a clean, sharp scalpel or razor blade and make a clean cut of the shoot taken off the donor plant. If using a rooting hormone, don't dip cuttings into original container as you could contaminate the whole bottle. Place a little bit of the rooting hormone in a small bowl or shot glass, then dip or roll the cutting into it, exposing for 10–30 seconds before inserting it into its rooting media.
- Feed cuttings with plain water until roots appear.
- Switch to a ¼-strength "bloom" nutrient formula after roots have started to appear. The higher phosphorus level in the bloom nutrient encourages root growth and lower level of nitrogen is perfect because too much nitrogen can stunt new roots.
- Don't over-saturate the growing media. Too-wet grow media doesn't allow air exchange in the root zone and will cause the roots to rot. Seedlings are particularly vulnerable: if they are too wet, they will rot where the stem meets the grow media and fall over–this is called "damping off".

Thoughts on Clones

No matter what anyone says, clones are never EXACTLY identical. How could they be? They start from different parts and heights of the donor plant. These different locations can have a significant effect on the clone's growth characteristics. Different cuttings will have different hormone and nutritional levels as well as having been exposed to different light levels which will affect their growth characteristics.

If there are any problems during the cloning process such as a loss of turgor pressure from drying out, the "recovered" clones won't yield nearly as much as proper clones. This loss can be massive – up to 40% in my experience. Damaged or poorly handled clones can lead to inconsistent yields, though this is almost never tracked/investigated or even remembered.

Clones must never be allowed to dry out. I learned this lesson firsthand a commercial grow facility that I ran. There was a power outage on the second weekend after I took over. Unfortunately, the facility was using aeroponic cloners at the time. The power dropped early Sunday morning and the outage was not discovered until hours later. The limited weekend staff were not prepared for such an event. It took several more hours to purchase and set up a generator. By the time the power was restored, the clones in the cloners had all wilted over.

The clones did visually bounce back, and management thought they were fine. I mentioned they would not produce nearly as much as clones that got off to a good start. When the harvest numbers came in, results from the damaged clones were about ~40% decreased from normal clone results – management was not happy.

The moral of the clone story is you need to have very healthy clones or your grow will not produce large harvests. Get over the "they'll grow through it" mentality. It simply does not work that way.

Tissue Culture

There is an alternative cloning technique called tissue culture that every serious grower should consider. Often also referred to as "micropropagation", tissue culture is the process of reproducing plants from small portions of the plant (stem, leave, node, etc.) These small pieces are grown in an agar based growth media.

The process starts of by mixing agar, plant hormones, sugar for a carbon source, and growth nutrients and then sterilizing the mixture. Hormones from the auxin family (also found in rooting compounds for use with clones) will result in a proliferation of roots, while hormones from the cytokinin family will produce shoots (branching). A balance of both auxin and cytokinin will produce unorganized growth called callus cells. These callus cells can be grown, divided and transplanted into a new growth media for either root or shoot production.

Both hobby and commercial growers can take advantage of tissue culture. For hobbyists, there is at least one company selling kits that include premade agar/hormone/sugar/nutrient mix ready for use in a tube. All you have to do is sterilize the plant part you're culturing and introduce it into the pre-sterilized agar mixture.

For the commercial growers, there are companies that design, build and provide training for tissue culture labs. These labs typically include air filtration through a laminar flow bench, media and plant preparation stations, an autoclave for sterilization, and racks and lights to grow the "plantlets".

Tissue culture has some unique advantages:

- The major advantage is that thousands of plants can be grown in the space that would otherwise occupies hundreds of clones. It is possible to culture multiple plantlets in a single baby food sized jar.
- Tissue culture requires significantly less light than traditional cloning. Plantlets are grown under 50-75 μmol m^{-2} s^{-1} vs. 75-125 μmol m^{-2} s^{-1} for clones.
- Another use for tissue culture is to "restore" genetics that have gotten infected. Plant growth nodes can grow faster than diseases and can be used to regenerate non-infected plants.
- No need to maintain mother plants.

Vegetative Growth with LEDs

Once your cuttings are fully rooted and hardened off, they need to be transplanted into the grow media in which they will do their vegetative growth–building their stems and nodes, increasing size, and preparing for flowering. To support this growth, light and CO_2 levels are increased. The plants are still tender, so watch your PPFD. The plants should have room to grow up toward the light, getting closer to it and thus increasing the light levels they receive as they get taller.

CO_2 supplementation is very effective in the vegetative cycle. By increasing the CO_2 concentration to approximately 1200 ppm (parts per million), you can shorten the length of time it takes to grow the plants to the desired height. They'll grow 20-30% faster than without supplementation, though CO_2 supplementation is not required for a great harvest. For the hobby growers don't worry if your setup won't allow for it. Just be sure you're correctly using ventilation to exchange the air in your grow room on a regular interval so that the CO_2 your plants consume is replenished from outside. Commercial growers definitely need to supplement with CO_2 during this stage of growth.

Depending on your growing system, you may need to transplant the plants into larger containers at some point in the vegetative cycle. Remember, big roots equal big harvests.

Flowering with LEDs

For short-day plants such as cannabis, once they have grown to the size you want, it's time to "flip" the photoperiod to induce flowering. This involves changing the photoperiod to a 12-hour-on/12-hour-off light cycle and increasing the light intensity for short day plants.

Shortening the light cycle will generate hormonal changes within the plants that trigger flowering. Cannabis will also "stretch" during this phase, increasing their vertical height by double to quadruple. Make sure to plan accordingly and switch into flowering before your plants are too tall–after the stretch, they still need to comfortably fit inside your grow space and maintain a proper distance from the light.

Make sure to rigidly maintain your 12-hours-on/12-hours-off lighting schedule once you enter the flowering cycle. *Once again, no matter what, don't expose your garden to light during the dark period.* Also–very important–if daylight savings time kicks in during the flowering phase, <u>don't reset your timers</u>. Wait until this grow is complete to change your timers. Some flowering plants react very negatively to even subtle changes in light schedules. It's too easy to make a mistake monkeying with the timer mid-grow that could cost you your entire harvest!

Keeping Donor/Mother Plants with LEDs

Keeping donor plants is very similar to the vegetative growth stage of plants that are intended to be flowered, with similar environmental and lighting requirements. The one major difference is the nutritional program for donor plants. These plants are being grown to produce cuttings, not flowers. In order to produce the best possible clones, the donor plants benefit from being fed a properly designed regimen.

 **Sloper Says**

Keep your best plant for a mother plant, not the weakest one that you don't want to flower. Healthy moms = healthy cuttings = healthy clones!

Overfed or improperly fed donor plants produce crummy clones, while properly fed donor plants will build up lots of stored carbohydrates, which are the energy source that cuttings will use for root production. Clones that don't have enough stored carbohydrates have a tougher time producing big, healthy roots. Closely watch donor plant nitrogen levels: too much, and the plant will have to use up its stored energy to process it. Too little, and the plant will become pale and weak. Also, be sure to include enough calcium, which is required to build strong cell walls.

Summary Grow Conditions

The table on the next page summarizes optimal environmental conditions for each stage of growth for commercial cannabis plants based on my experience. Over the years I've learned cannabis can process much more light than most people grow under. We know from the Stark-Einstein Law that the more light we deliver to our plants the more harvestable bud weight we will grow.

The people I've taught this "high light methodology" to have become extremely good growers, producing significantly larger harvests than their rivals. There are growers that are going to say that this is too much light in flower… all I have to say is, maybe it is <u>for them</u>. To be successful with intense flowering light levels

REQUIRES you have very healthy plants going into the flower room that have been grown under proper PPFD levels, and that you provide them with enough nutrition (more on proper plant nutrition in chapter 9).

	DLI (mol day^{-1})	PPFD (µmol m^{-2} s^{-1})	Leaf Temp (°F/°C)	CO2 (PPM)	Humidity (%)	Light Cycle (hr.)
Mothers	32.4 - 38.9	400-700	80-83/27-28	400*-800	55-70	18 on, 6 off
Clones	4.8 – 8.1	75-125	78-82/26-28	400*	75-90	18 on, 6 off
Early Veg	13.0-19.4	200-300	80-83/27-28	800-1200	55-70	18 on, 6 off
Late Veg	35.6-45.4	450-600	80-83/27-28	1000-1200	55-70	18 on, 6 off
Early Flower	34.6-43.2	750-1000	80-83/27-28	1000-1200	55-65	12 on, 12 off
Mid Flower	38.9-56.1	900-1300	80-83/27-28	1200-1500	50-60	12 on, 12 off
Late Flower	51.8-64.8	1200-1500	80-83/27-28	1200-1500	45-55	12 on, 12 off

Transpiration

Plants use the process of transpiration to cool themselves. It's essentially the same as an evaporative cooler at your home or office. The heat energy from the plant is transferred to the water molecules emitted through the stomata, take the heat energy with them. This is why the temperature of the leaves are a ~3°F/2°C cooler than the surrounding air.

In addition to cooling, transpiration is used to transfer some minerals within the plant. Water emitted by the stomata creates a kind of a "pump" within the plant which moves water to maintain turgor pressure. Calcium and boron are effectively "pulled" through the plant via the transpiration process. This is a passive event with the nutrients being relocated via the transpiration process. Having plants that are properly transpiring is critical to having healthy plants.

Vapor Pressure Deficit

When I published the second edition of this book in 2017, I debated whether to include the topic of **vapor pressure deficit (VPD)**. At the time I felt there was much more to focus on and considered VPD to be a distraction. Flash forward to late 2019 and suddenly everyone in the cannabis industry is talking about VPD as if it's some sort of superhero that can save us from humidity woes. VPD describes the difference in water pressure within the plant aka "turgor pressure" compared to the surrounding environment. The difference between them is the "deficit".

In reality, the greenhouse community has been discussing VPD for a long time. As the adult use of cannabis has become legal in many of the United States, Canada and Uruguay, more of it is being cultivated in greenhouses. This is most likely the reason for the sudden mainstream discussion and use of VPD in the cannabis industry.

VPD is a method of determining optimum humidity and temperature for each stage of plant growth. It considers air and leaf temperatures instead of simply relying on relative humidity to make predictions about a garden environment. VPD is a helpful guideline for predicting disease threat, condensation potential, and irrigation needs in addition to helping to maintain plant health in all stages of life.

EXPERT CORNER

Relative Humidity (RH) and VPD are inversely related. As RH increases, VPD decreases.

Keep in mind the research that determined optimum VPD values did not include cannabis as a test plant. It's likely that current "general" VPD guidelines hold true for cannabis, but as always determine what works for you, in your location down to the specific grow room. VPD guidelines should not be considered absolute but rather a guide to general starting points.

Current commonly recommended VPD's for cannabis are:

- Propagation / Early Veg = 0.4 – 0.8 kPa
- Late Veg / Early Flower = 0.8 – 1.2 kPa
- Mid / Late Flower = 1.2 – 1.6 kPa

There are plenty of VPD calculators available online. Make sure to find one that includes both leaf and air temperature in addition to humidity. Some do not include leaf temperature measurements (or make assumptions for you). Additionally, be careful to understand what units of measure are being used or you can get confused really fast. The cannabis community typically uses Kilopascals (kPa) and sometimes millibars (mbar). In case you need to convert, 1 mbar = 0.1 kPa.

In my experience, leaf surface temperatures under LED grow lights are ~3°F/2°C cooler than the surrounding air due to cooling from transpiration.

Maintaining the Environment

Maintaining a healthy indoor environment is probably the most critical factor to garden success. I can't stress this enough. You can have the best plant genetics, space-age plant nutrition, and the greatest LED grow light ever, but if your environment is off, it will cost you in terms of quantity and quality. Heat-stressed, too dry, or otherwise deficient gardens just don't perform well.

For each stage of a plant's life cycle, there are suggested optimum environmental conditions. The three basic environmental factors for any garden–indoors or out–are temperature, humidity, and CO_2 level. All three of these variables need to be at their optimum level for a garden to perform its best.

For the hobby grower, don't worry if you can't get to these exact figures–they are *recommendations* to you, not exact requirements. We all have to deal with the real environment in our grow spaces and may not be able to pay for all the equipment needed to overcome its challenges.

For the commercial grower, there is no reason not to be able to maintain a proper grow environment. Bad planning and lack of funds are not going to cut it today. We have the technology; it simply costs money to purchase and operate.

HVAC systems for commercial grow facilities need to be designed by experts. Take advantage of their skills and don't take shortcuts. Although there are some rules of thumb, commercial HVAC is ridiculously complex. Here's a quick rundown on how to create optimal conditions in your garden and how to make corrections if these factors are out of spec.

 Sloper Says

Don't spend too much time trying to "chase the number" on your thermometer/hygrometer. Instead, use the thermometer/ hygrometer as a reference, watch your plants, and only intervene when there are problems.

Too Hot

Just like humans, plants suffer if the garden is too hot. Plants have evolved mechanisms to help them with too hot conditions: in the presence of sufficient water, plants cool themselves by opening their stomata and releasing water molecules that cool the plant as they evaporate. Plants can also reorient the angle of their leaves limiting their exposure to light. Both of these solutions require the plant to spend its energy defending itself instead of producing fruits and flowers. Additionally, chemical reactions inside a plant, including photosynthesis, depend on enzymes that operate best at optimal temperatures and might stop working altogether outside of their target range.

What's too hot? In general, gardens thrive in the same conditions people do. Daytime temperatures should not exceed upper 80's°F (low 30's°C). To cool the grow space, consider these options:

- Commercial grows use professionally-designed HVAC systems to maintain proper temperatures. Fans in these facilities circulate the air not to cool the space.
- Fans are the most cost-effective heat-removing tool for a hobby garden. If the exhaust fan does not provide adequate cooling, consider adding an intake fan. Actively bringing air into the garden reduces back pressure on the exhaust fan and allows more air to flow out. If that doesn't reduce temperatures enough, consider buying a bigger exhaust fan. Both of these techniques assume that the outside air is cooler than the desired garden temperature.
- Hobbyists should use an air conditioner if fans are not enough. Since air conditioners are expensive to operate, look for ones with high SEER (Seasonal Energy Efficiency Ratio) ratings. If you're supplementing with CO_2, be sure to use an A/C that separates the room air from the exhaust air–such as a "dual hose" unit or a "mini-split".

Too Cold

Too cold is one problem HID gardeners rarely encounter. While excess heat is a perpetual threat to the HID garden, LED gardens can get too cold, even during the light cycle. Extended periods of daytime temperatures below 75°F/24°C can stunt growth and shrink harvests. Too cold isn't generally much of a problem during the summer, but it can be a serious challenge in winter, depending on where you live. To warm the grow space, consider these options:

- A well designed commercial HVAC system will include heat as well as A/C.
- Heaters are useful, though they draw a significant amount of electricity. When using a heater with a fan, be careful to not blow hot air directly onto the plants or you can burn them or dry them out. Oil-filled radiator-style heaters are better, as they radiate heat into the room without blowing it around.
- Hobbyists should use a fan speed controller to automatically speed up or slow down the exhaust fan based on room temperature. Fan speed controllers are a cost-effective alternative to expensive environmental controllers. Choose a controller that changes the fan's rotation based on temperature: lower temperature = slower fan speed. This helps retain existing heat in the grow space.
- If the grow is too cold and the area immediately outside of the grow space is warmer, crack the door open during the light cycle to let some of the warm outside air mix in with the cooler air in the garden. This strategy may not work in commercial grows supplement CO_2.
- Consider using a backdraft dampener to prevent any unwanted airflow into the garden through stopped intake or exhaust fans.

Absolute vs. Relative Humidity

Absolute humidity is the amount of water vapor in the air regardless of air temperature. It's measured in grams of water per cubic meter (g/m3). As a reference, warm air at 86°F/30°C has the capacity to retain 30 grams of water vapor per cubic meter. Cold air at a temperature of 32°F/0°C only retains 5 grams of water vapor in the same cubic meter.

Relative humidity is also a measurement of the moisture in the air but in this case, it is relative to the air temperature. It's a measurement of the water vapor in the air vs. total water holding capacity of the air. Relative humidity of 50% means the air is carrying half the potential water vapor possible at that temperature. Relative humidity is what is reported on weather stations/channels and affects how we "feel" about the temperature of the air.

Too Humid

Proper humidity is just as important to successful gardening as proper temperatures. People often ask me how much humidity will my plants produce? The answer is simple: since plants transpire up to 97% of the water they take in, as a rule of thumb, assume they transpire 100% of the water they are fed. Planning for worst case, not the best case is required.

When your garden is too humid, it is at risk of attack by fungus and mold that can ruin or contaminate your harvest. Fungus is very hard to kill and multiplies exponentially, so every hour matters. In addition, when it's overly humid, the plants have more difficulty transpiring. "Too humid" varies stages of growth and changes throughout the life of the plants. Refer to the "Summary Grow Conditions" chart above or VPD calculations.

To reduce humidity, try one of these tactics:

- Dehumidifiers physically remove unwanted humidity from the air by blowing air across chilled plates or coils that condense water vapor in the air into water, which is collected in a vessel or drained out via plumbing.
- Dehumidifiers for commercial grows should be specified and installed by a qualified HVAC professional. These units are sized based on the size of the facility and volume of water to be removed from the air, stated as pints or litters per day.

- If you're battling high temperatures, use a water-cooled dehumidifier instead of a "heat pump" model. Water-cooled units blow room-temperature air across a coil that's chilled by pumping cold water through it.
- For the hobbyists, if the air outside of the garden is dryer than the garden air, increase the number of air exchanges in your grow space by beefing up your ventilation system. This works best when outside air is about the same temperature as the air in your grow space–if not, you may need to find ways to correct garden temperature after bringing in more outside air.
- Air conditioners dry out the air as a by-product of cooling it, solving two problems if your garden is also too hot. Just make sure you have a plan to remove and dispose of the water that condenses out of the air conditioner, as hobby scale units can produce water that is fairly acidic or contaminated with metals. Don't use it to water living plants–it should be treated and reused or disposed down the drain if treatment is not possible. Some commercial units allow for the re-use of the water.

Too Dry

Too dry can be just as devastating as too humid for some plants–the plants close their stomata to protect themselves, shutting themselves down and slowing growth. Generally, this is more of a problem under HID lights than LEDs because of the excess heat produced by HIDs.

While more research on the topic is required, LED-grown plants seem to have a wider humidity tolerance than plants grown under other lights.

To raise humidity, consider these techniques:

- Commercial grow facilities use dry fogging systems to raise humidity. They create humidity by pressurizing water through a nozzle with the aid of compressed air to produce a fine fog that does not settle on surfaces before evaporating.
- Humidifiers used in hobby gardens spray fine water droplets into the air. The more expensive ultrasonic models spray a cool, fine mist in contrast to the large water droplets that impeller-style units spray out. With humidifiers, you get what you pay for: ultrasonic units are more expensive and require *very* clean water but raise the room's humidity more effectively than impeller units, without leaving water puddles wherever they stand
- Another solution for the hobby gardener is to hang one or more wet towels. In a small grow room, this can provide instant relief for a dry spell. This is a short-term solution–the towels must always be damp and so must be checked or changed several times a day. To prevent humidity buildup when the light is off, either let the towels dry out late in the day or remove them before the lights go out.

Low CO_2

Plants use the carbon from CO_2 as the building blocks of plant structures as well as a fuel source from the carbohydrates created by photosynthesis. It is important to maintain the CO_2 levels or growth will slow or stop completely.

Plants require some air movement to make sure there is enough CO_2 directly available to absorb. Plants can actually draw <u>all</u> the CO_2 out of the boundary layer, the air that's directly surrounding the leaf, even when CO_2 levels are enriched. With gentle air flow, the CO_2 within the boundary layer can be constantly replaced.

There are several ways to maintain or increase the amount of CO_2 in your garden. Commercial and some hobbyists supplement CO_2 using tanks or generators. Hobby growers may also use organic/chemical CO_2 emitters even rely on the intake/exhaust fans. If you supplement with CO_2, be sure to dispense the gas as high in the room as possible. CO_2 is denser than air so it will fall down on the plants. Releasing CO_2 at the same level as the plants may cause it to be wasted when it falls to the floor and stays there instead of contacting the plants' leaves where the photosynthetic magic happens.

Here are a few points to consider when it comes to maintaining or increasing CO_2 in your garden:

- The most common way to add CO_2 to your garden environment is to inject it from a pressurized tank.
- Commercial operations typically have large CO_2 storage tanks on their property that get refilled by a supplier, often the company who sold/installed the system.
- CO_2 tanks for hobbyists can be purchased at retail hydroponic shops and either exchanged at the shop when they are empty or refilled at a commercial gas distributor. CO_2 tanks need to be pressure checked every five years by law; check the inspection date stamped into the shoulder of the tank to be sure that it's "in-date". You'll also need a regulator for the tank, a timer or an electronic CO_2 controller to control the CO_2 release and maintain an appropriate CO_2 concentration, and a distribution system to scatter the CO_2 across the garden.
- CO_2 generators release CO_2 into the garden as a by-product of burning propane or natural gas. These units contain gas burner jets inside an insulated housing and when properly used present very little fire hazard. The gas burners are tuned to produce CO_2–safe carbon dioxide–rather than CO–dangerous carbon monoxide, which is a normal by-product of burning fossil fuels. While there is a risk that these units will produce a least a little CO, a dangerous accumulation in the garden is unlikely as long as the garden's ventilation system functions properly and the generator is in good working order. Be sure to put a CO alarm in your garden so you can identify CO buildup and take corrective action before the problem becomes dangerous to you and your plants. While you're at it, put up a smoke alarm or combination smoke/CO alarm, and put a fire extinguisher in or near the garden.
- CO_2 generators can also produce ethylene, which is a plant hormone and can negatively affect plants. It's commonly used to ripen green tomatoes in transit. Keep an eye on your plants and if they begin to suffer instead of thriving, cease CO_2 supplementation and have your generator checked.
- Compost and chemical bags are small buckets of mushroom compost or bags of chemicals that slowly release CO_2. Again position the outlet for these products as high in the garden as possible. Compost and chemical CO_2 generators are gaining in popularity for small gardens that don't have space for additional equipment, though the low CO_2 production of some of them makes one wonder "why bother"? Try these buckets/bags if you're ready to experiment with CO_2 in a small garden, and see whether they help. It's likely that you'll need a CO_2 tank or burner along with a quality CO_2 environmental controller if you want to take the best advantage of supplemental CO_2 in your garden.
- For small gardens, exhaust fans not only remove heat, they also replenish CO_2 by bringing fresh outside air into the garden in a grow space with suitable air intake. This should ensure an adequate supply of fresh CO_2 and is the best option for small gardeners who don't want to fuss with CO_2 tanks or generators.

HID-to-LED Conversion

The number one most asked question I get asked from growers that are considering making "the switch" to LED grow lights is "Can you tell me *exactly* what I need to change to be successful with LEDs"? Simply, *no*. It would very difficult to come up with a conversion chart–believe me, I've tried. Gardening, especially indoors, is very personal. What works for one grower might be a total fail for another.

One tip is to remember what we learned about RuBisCO. Whatever temperatures you grow under with HIDs, warm the room up a few degrees when you convert to LEDs. If plants are cooler than their optimal temperature, their growth rate will slow down. Start by increasing garden air temperature 3-6°F/2-4°C above your usual HID air temperatures to offset lower heat generated by the LED grow light, and then experiment from there.

A/C Performance: LED vs. HID

HIDs generate different demands on air conditioners than LEDs. HIDs create light through blackbody radiation. This means they superheat plasma to the point where it glows and gives off photons. HIDs come up to full heat output fairly quickly (approximately 10-15 min), which does not leave much time for the A/C to respond. The A/C is in a sense "behind" the heat being generated so it has to "chase" the heat load. This can add considerable stress and shorten the useful life of the A/C unit.

LEDs don't heat up nearly as fast: typically they take 30-60 min to completely warm up. This slower heat introduction allows the A/C to respond and control the heat more in alignment with its design. The diagrams below should make this difference clear. Notice the increased A/C usage in the HID system, as well as the significantly greater ambient temperature correction it has to correct.

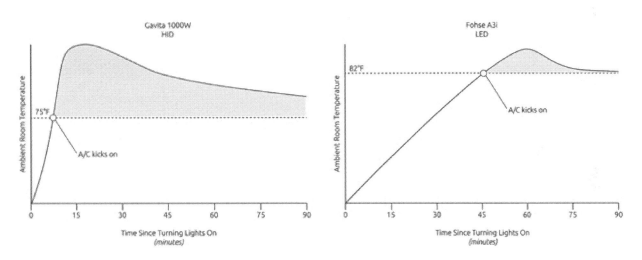

Changes in Dehumidification Strategy

As previously discussed, plants can transpire 97% of the water they absorb through their root system. For a large plant (5+ feet) that can be a whole bunch of water. Other activities such as hand watering can introduce additional humidity due to the inherent wastefulness of the process—especially in a large commercial facility with thousands of plants in a single room.

Many growers rely on their A/C to assist in dehumidification of the grow space. Although this strategy might work for HID-lit rooms, depending on A/C for dehumidification can create problems in LED rooms, especially in the winter. Warmer room temperatures are required to stimulate photosynthesis under LEDs (remember RuBisCO!), so the A/C should run less. Which means less dehumidification. Even though warmer air will hold more water, it's usually not enough to offset the difference.

If you are converting an existing HID grow room to LEDs, you will most likely need to increase your dehumidification capacity. I've seen LED conversions that require twice the amount of dehumidification capacity vs. HID grow rooms. I recommend working with both a knowledgeable grow consultant and an HVAC specialist (ideally with plant experience) when converting from HID to LED, in order to get the room's humidity right from the start.

HID vs. LED Side-By-Side Trials

In the early days of LED grow lights, growers wanted to see both lighting technologies go head to head in a side-by-side trial. It was one of those "prove it works" situations. Even I advocated these trials in my 2008 Growing Edge International magazine article on LED grow lights, unfortunately such a trial can be rigged for either side to win, by plant temperature alone.

Say you wanted HID to win: cool the room down. Since the HID side produces lots of excess heat, it can buffer itself on temperature while the cold will drive the LED side below optimum temperatures thus reducing the LED yield. Conversely, if you wanted the LED to win, heat the room up. This will cause the HID side to go way above optimum temperatures, reducing yield and potentially quality while the LED side should be fine—LED gardens can typically survive temperatures into the low 90's without much loss in production.

In addition to the differences in environmental conditions needed by HID vs. LED gardens, there is a possibility of light pollution from the HID side adding to the results on the LED side since HID have low target efficiency, thus "leaking" photons onto the LED side. This is another reason the results of LED vs. HID trials might not be valid.

Light Maps

As the indoor horticultural industry matures, perspective commercial grow light purchasers are getting savvier. Large commercial lighting sales require "light maps" which are generated by computer modeling. In a perfect world, these light maps would accurately describe where every photon will land but that's not what they do. Light design programs like DIALux are focused on how much light will be reflected into human eyes off of different surfaces in the room, road, or parking lot. They take into consideration light levels directly delivered to the eye, but proper lighting design steers light away from the eyes in the first place. They were NOT designed for horticultural purposes even though that's how they are being used.

Light maps make great sales tools. They are impressive, especially to the untrained eye. Be careful how much you believe light maps as there are lots of factors that can be manipulated. The number and location of calculation points can be chosen to make grow lights look extremely intense with near-perfect uniformity. The reflective nature of the surfaces can be adjusted altering outcomes more than you would think. Unscrupulous LED grow light manufacturers can manipulate these and other factors in their favor. What ultimately matters is the quantity (with a small consideration towards wavelength) of photons hitting the canopy of your grow.

All current light mapping software measures in foot candles (lumens) and candelas per square meter (lux) and need a correction factor applied to generate results in PPFD. This is another "adjustment" point that can be used to produce a result that is favorable to the seller. The correction factor is calculated from the number and type of LED emitters used in the fixture. For an LED grow light that contains cool white and warm white with a small percentage of deep red (660nm) emitters, the correction factor from foot candles to PPFD is ~0.18-0.20.

.IES/.LDT Files

In addition to light modeling software, generating a light map requires some information about the fixture(s) that will be used in the grow room. These "photometric data files" used by lighting design applications are created with the aid of a **goniophotometer**. A goniophotometer measures light output at 855 different angles while rotating the source, creating the file measuring where each photon is cast.

For North America, in 1986 IESNA created the standard LM-63-86, "IES Recommended Standard File Format for Electronic Transfer of Photometric Data". You can easily recognize these files as they use ".ies" filename extension. For Europe, EULUMDAT is the industry standard photometric data file. These files use ".ldt" as their filename extension.

"PAR Map"

PAR map is a bad term that has recently shown up in the cannabis industry as an alternative to light maps. Maybe I'm being picky but considering that PAR is simply a definition of 400-700nm wavelengths, it's like saying "show me the 400-700nm map". How do the so-called maps know the photons being emitted from the fixture are all in the PAR range? What about non-PAR signaling wavelengths? We also know from Chapter 3 that PAR does not tell the whole story, especially about photomorphogenesis. The term PAR Map is just sloppy, no matter how you look at it.

LEDs and Reduced Cannabis Flowering Time

In the early days of LED grow lights, several manufacturers made wild claims that their lights could reduce the flowering time because of their "perfect spectrum". I say PROVE IT with real analytical data. No one has done any proper scientific trials on this topic, so no one knows for sure. Research may unlock some morphological mysteries through spectrum manipulation but we're not there yet... not even close.

Cannabis (and other short-day plants) do not begin flowering on the first day you change the light schedule to 12/12. Cannabis plants have to go through complex hormonal changes before they actually start the flowering process. Minimizing stress during this transition might be the key to shortening flowering times. Under LEDs, you have a similar (or often exactly the same) spectrum in both veg and flower. I've speculated that it's similar spectrum not perfect spectrum that could be the reason some LED grow light manufacturers claim decreased flowering times. Unfortunately we don't have any empirical data to back that theory up either.

You can harvest cannabis a few days to a week earlier if you're inclined, though this is a bad idea as cannabinoid development happens in the last few weeks of the flowering cycle. Harvesting a week early can cut up to a third of the cannabinoid production time which translates to a major loss the total cannabinoid oil weight.

Is Dimming Needed?

In the last edition of this book I posed the question is dimming needed. I mentioned it was OK for hobby gardens but not needed in commercial facilities. This is another place I have changed my thinking. I've toured a countless number of grow facilities in my cultivation career. With the exception of a few, most of them had serious issues with their plants. The trouble started with run out genetics with rock hard purple stems. This chain starts with poor donor plants, which became crummy clones, that didn't veg well, and ultimately could not handle much light in flower.

There is no way plants cultivated this way can handle heavy photon densities. At the cost of harvest weight, the only thing the growers can do with plants like this is dim the lights. Without the ability dim they would have to raise the lights (if possible) or suffer the consequences.

Inrush Current

Inrush is the instantaneous current load when electronic devices turn on. Devices with power supplies often draw more power when they initially turn on, then decrease over a few seconds to their normal current loads. Think of it as the extra power they need to charge themselves up. The quality of the driver in the LED grow lights will dictate if there will be problems with inrush current. Cheaper lights can be prone to this phenomenon.

Dimming may help solve inrush current issues. With the aid of a controller, the lights can be turned on in a dimmed state and slowly increased over a few seconds to minutes. This strategy will lower the initial current draw.

7: Planning the Grow Space

Up until now, we've focused on LED grow lights: where they came from, why they are great for indoor gardening, the lights themselves, and how to use them. That's a lot in a short time, but there's still more. Now let's put most of the technical and industry stuff behind us and focus on creating a thriving indoor garden—one that produces the highest-quality crop you can muster.

While this chapter was primarily written for the hobby growing community each of the topics is still relevant in a commercial grow. So you pros should give it as least a skim. Commercial grow facilities are getting larger and complex with every passing month. It takes lots of experts working together to design one. There are engineering firms that can assist but make sure you vet them well. Since legal cannabis is very new, the firms have little to no experience in designing grow facilities. My advice is to get references and contact them to discuss the firms work. I can tell stories for days about the simple mistakes made by engineering firms without cannabis experience that led to huge headaches for the grow teams.

Plan

What first? Make a plan, make a plan, make a plan. Your plan should include these things:

- A budget including a list of items you need to buy and operating expenses such as rent, utilities, genetics, grow media and nutrients. Include the specific sizes of various items of equipment, such as your grow trays, light(s), fans, etc. with estimated prices.
- A physical drawing of your grow space, both from above (for laying out the physical placement of items within the space) and from the side (to check that the equipment you're using will fit in the vertical height of the space).
- A lighting plan: even if you're only hanging one light in a closet, it's always "illuminating" to carefully consider the light needs of your crop and how you will satisfy those inside your grow space.
- An environmental plan, based on controlling humidity, temperature and CO_2 refreshment, as well as air movement within the grow facility.
- A nutrient (or "wet") plan, starting with what grow system(s) will you use? How will you provide nutrient solution/water to your plants and/or reservoirs? How will you deal with nutrient runoff? Carefully consider how far and how many times you or your staff will carry water, it's heavy.
- An electrical plan which stipulates how all electric/electronic devices in the grow space will be safely connected to power, as well as any backup power supplies that may be needed.
- An operating strategy: what are your plans for pest management, light/dark cycles? How will you secure the grow?

Budget

Before you begin to build or reconfigure an LED grow room, you must have a budget. There's a lot of equipment to buy, and if you need to make any physical changes to your grow space, those could be costly.

Figuring out a good starting point for your budget can be tricky—hobby grow spaces can cost from hundreds to thousands of dollars, depending on equipment and configuration while commercial operations can run into the 10's to 100's of millions.

Your budget should allow for the purchase of high-quality LED light(s), ventilation/HVAC equipment, humidifiers/dehumidifiers controllers/timers, a grow system for the plants, and a host of accessories. The rest of this chapter will help you decide what equipment you need.

Armed with this information, take some time to research average prices for the products you desire at your local indoor gardening centers, online and/or from commercial suppliers. Don't forget to add in any applicable local sales tax, which can be as high as 10%, plus shipping if you're buying products from online retailers.

Sloper Says

Based on my experience working with new indoor gardeners in my former hydroponics shops, it's likely that you will have to make changes during your first run, so don't spend all of your money up front.

Once you've reached a tentative budget for your grow space, add 20% to 25% to account for smaller details (such as fittings, tubing, and chains) as well as changes you may have to make once you're dealing in real, three-dimensional space. It's just about guaranteed that you will have to make changes, potentially lots of them if you didn't do enough homework, so it's best to account for this in your budget.

Different nutrients, quieter fans, additional controllers, and other unexpected needs always seem to crop up when lighting up a new grow space—even if you're an experienced indoor gardener. These problems will typically show up after the plants begin growing, so be warned and be ready.

Grow Space Drawing

Drawing out the garden's design on paper, whether by hand or using a computer-aided design (CAD) program, will help you to discover many important things you might otherwise overlook.

A View from Above and Beside

Start by drawing a bird's eye view of the grow space including walls, doors, windows, electrical outlets, plumbing features (sinks/drains) and any other features or obstacles that affect how the space can be used.

Next draw in the equipment you plan to use that stands on the floor—grow systems, reservoirs, filters and so forth—allowing for aisles between rows and/or access from the side for tending the plants. When positioning your grow systems, consider the next layer up—the systems need to be placed below where the grow lights shine. Design the lighting as a separate layer, then reposition the grow systems as needed.

Once you're comfortable with your grow space floor plan, draw out what it will look like from the side. Plan for any equipment that stands on the floor, plus any equipment hung or mounted above such as grow lights, ducting, fans or filters. Include any equipment that may be in the middle such as sensors, controllers and timers. Ultimately this may require drawing more than one side view. Be sure to stay within any vertical height limits… then tweak until done.

Be Realistic About the Number of Plants

My number one piece of planning advice: be realistic about how much you can grow. One of the biggest mistakes new gardeners make is cramming in too many plants. Plants need enough space between them so that their leaves don't touch or minimally touch.

This allows air and light to flow down into the plants and completely surround them. In nature, dominant plants tend to crowd out smaller, weaker ones, and the same is true indoors. Give your plants enough space so they can all get along and grow strong. As a general rule of thumb smaller cannabis plants need ~2 sq. ft and large ones can take up 4+.

Plant Access

Remember that the grow space can't entirely be dedicated to plants. You need space for timers, fans, filters, and irrigation systems plus aisles to work in. You should make sure that the gardener(s) working in the grow can physically reach every plant. This might sound silly but consider the depth of the plant spaces you're designing versus the length of your arm. You can't tend to your plants if you can't reach them.

Hobbyists should consider building or purchasing a grow box or tent with back or side doors that allow you to extend the area occupied by plants all the way to the edges, increasing productive space without increasing grow space size. Rows of plants in commercial grows and one-sided grow spaces such as a bedroom closet should not be wider than three feet, unless you plan to grow longer arms!

Lighting Plan

After your physical grow space, the most important thing about any indoor garden is the light. After all, it's what allows us to garden without the sun. Below are a few things to consider regarding your grow lights that may affect your grow space plan.

Light Height for Non-Dimmable Lights

Proper light height is key and the only real way to get it right is with a quantum meter. What should the hobby growers without the budget to purchase one do?

Start by consulting your LED grow light manufacturer's light map, then give yourself at least 25% extra above the light so you can move it up if necessary as well as provide space for mounting electrical cords and the like. Then watch your garden and let it tell you if the light is too high or too low. If the manufacturer of the light you're considering can't or won't help with light height, find another grow light vendor.

Light Leaks

For a garden that contains light-sensitive plants, you must ensure that your grow space is 100% light tight. Completely cover any external windows with foam board or other light-blocking material. Seal doors with press-on foam weather stripping; choose low-density foam, as it compresses well and does not add very much resistance to closing the door. If you're in a large room or warehouse, consider building a "blind" or vestibule inside the door that allows you to open and close the external door without affecting lighting inside the grow.

When installing air intake vents, make sure they don't allow light to enter the garden along with air. Strategies to overcome this potential light source include:

- Making PVC light traps. These consist of at least two 90-degree PVC elbows twisted together; light can't travel around that many square corners.
- Using darkroom louver vents, which can be purchased at photography supply companies.

If you build your own light traps, paint the inside matte black, as this will reduce the amount of light that reflects inside the trap and will help to keep light contained within the trap.

Mounting/Hanging the Lights

This next section offers advice aimed directly at smaller sized gardens. This could be a hobby garden or a small test garden at a large grow facility.

Perforated Angle Iron

Anyone who mounts their lights to the ceiling or top panel of a grow box or space has been there: looking up, drill in hand, swearing this will be the last time they move the grow light–this time it will finally be in the perfect spot. There is a better solution: perforated angle iron. Available at most home improvement centers, perforated angle iron is a long piece of metal bent to a 90-degree angle with holes every inch or so along its length.

Attach lengths of perforated angle iron in the ceiling of your grow room, or on both walls near the ceiling, with appropriate mounting screws/anchors to hold the weight of your light(s). For multiple or heavy lights, if you're in a room instead of a grow box, attach the angle iron to the ceiling rafters or wall studs.

Then when you're trying out different light configurations, you can just hang the lights from the predrilled holes using cables and clips instead of drilling new holes and installing new hooks and anchors for every lighting change. Be sure to use secure attachments when hanging grow lights from perforated angle iron such as chains, metal carabiners or heavy-duty zip-ties.

Racks/Stands

Grow spaces with high ceilings may require a method to mount lights lower and closer to the garden's canopy. There are many racking systems appropriate for grow facilities, some support multiple layers as required for vertical farming.

There are also metal grow stands which support 4x4' or 4x8' grow trays, with space below for equipment or a reservoir, and one or more metal extensions above the tray for hanging a grow light(s). These are generally targeted to smaller grows and can be bought or ordered from hydroponic stores and garden centers.

Custom built stand systems are popular an option and are generally made from 2x4's screwed together. An advantage of custom built systems is that they can be configured to exactly fit the space.

Light Movers

Light movers multiply your grow light's effective "reach" into your garden. Think about it for a moment: does the sun suddenly turn on directly overhead in the morning? Does it turn off exactly in the same position at night?

In nature, the sun rises in the east and sets in the west, but in our gardens, the "sun" turns on directly overhead and at full intensity. The sun's natural daily course across the sky provides outdoor plants with morning and evening side lighting as well as high-noon direct top lighting.

When your grow light moves across the garden on a light mover, the light can reach deeper into plants' leaves and stems instead of just the leaves on top. It does not take too much movement to create this effect–moving the light as little as a few inches can significantly increase the amount of light that finds its way further into the garden's canopy, which will increase yields.

Light movers are popular with hobby growers. These gardens are small, typically with one or possibly two lights. On the other hand, commercial grows do not use them. The light mover in a commercial setting is the light next to the light directly above the plants.

Environment/Air Flow Plan

Planning adequate air flow and environmental control into your grow space design is essential. Thoughtful environmental planning ensures that adequate amounts of CO_2 are available for the plants to convert to carbohydrates and helps to prevent fungus and mold infestations from becoming established.

Intake/Exhaust Fan Sizing

There are so many "rules of thumb" about how to calculate the proper intake and exhaust fan size that it can make your head spin. Most formulas call for enough ventilation to change the air in the grow space on a regular interval ranging from once every five minutes to twice a minute. While these formulas are a good start, they do not consider all the reasons a grower needs to ventilate his or her grow space: to remove heat, control humidity, and refresh CO_2 in grow room air (if the grower is not supplementing CO_2).

There is no exact formula for how much ventilation capacity your garden needs that makes much sense in the real world every time. Every garden is different–the length of ducting runs and the number of twists and bends in the ducting will dramatically affect the ability of your exhaust fan to push (or pull) air through the system. Carbon filters add additional, and considerable, restrictive back pressure–further limiting air flow and thereby increasing required fan size.

Start by determining your grow room's size in cubic feet by multiplying the room's length x width x height. A 4-by-4-by-7-foot room, for example, contains 112 cubic feet (4 x 4 x 7). You can use this number as a starting point to select a fan–you will need one that moves at least 112 CFM (cubic feet per minute) of air. Assuming that the air ducting and filter you're using with this fan create enough back pressure to reduce effective airflow through the system by half, this fan should allow for one complete garden air exchange every two minutes.

EXPERT CORNER

Buy an exhaust fan that is one size larger than you think you need and then use a fan speed controller to slow it down. This lets you exercise greater control over your garden's air quality—a larger fan can always be turned down, but you can't speed up a smaller one.

If your ventilation design includes long ducting runs and bends, particularly 90-degree bends, you'll need a bigger fan to overcome increased back pressure in the system. Unfortunately, the best advice is to go up at least one size (such as from a 6-to-8-inch fan) and see what happens. When it comes to ventilation fans, bigger is generally better. Your particular environment will dictate when this is necessary.

This fan sizing advice assumes you're using fans that can handle back pressure and that you're bringing enough replacement air into the garden through vents. Inline fans for gardening can move lots of air with minimum wall watts consumed, are tolerant of moderate back pressure, and come in sizes starting at 4 inches and going up to 16-inch-plus fans that look like small jet engines. If you're unsure what type of size fan to use, a local indoor garden center or commercial supplier should be able to help you correctly size your intake and exhaust fans.

Be sure that your environmental plan allows enough air to *enter* the grow space: drawing lots of air out of the garden without replacing that air can increase back pressure on the system and reduce fan efficiency. Darkroom louver vents are great for air intake but are restrictive, so make sure to size them correctly–here again, bigger rather than smaller will help to ensure there is enough air coming into the room. If you're unsure what size louver vent to use, contact the manufacturer to help purchase the correct size based on your airflow needs.

If you can't install passive air intake vents, or if you still need more incoming air after you've installed as many intake vents as you can, you'll need to force replacement air into the grow space with an air intake fan–but don't overdo it.

If your intake fan is more powerful than your exhaust fan, you may wind up forcing your garden's air out through the cracks in the room instead of through the filter. That could be a problem if you're trying to contain garden smells–some crops and fertilizers smell strongly, and you don't want to "skunk" your home or neighborhood with unpleasant smells.

The ideal ventilation setup has a slight amount of back pressure causing a negative pressure environment in the grow room–slightly less air entering than being drawn out. This will ensure that all the air and smells travel through the filter on the way out. You'll know you have it right when there is a little resistance to opening the grow room door. If an outward swinging door is difficult to open or an inward door flies open due to the exhaust fan running, that's a signal of inadequate "makeup" air.

Sealed Room

Unlike outdoor gardeners, indoor gardeners have the opportunity to supplement their garden's air with CO_2. If you're planning to supplement with CO_2, make sure your grow room can be sealed tight. Obviously, a grow tent is less desirable for a CO_2-enriched garden, since the gas would seep out of its many seams, zippers, and gussets. In grow rooms and grow boxes, use foam weather stripping to seal access doors, and "finger caulk" (often sold as "rope caulk" or "cord weather-stripping") to fill in small gaps. Finger caulk is a rubbery material that comes in narrow strips, does not dry, and can be rolled and formed to fit into small places. Powered air vents and backdraft dampeners are also great tools to prevent CO_2 loss.

EXPERT CORNER

CO_2 is one of the heavier components of air, so it settles. A small fan placed on the floor can stir up the CO_2 that has settled below your plants.

Sealing even small leaks can save on CO_2 costs. Do everything you can to close the room's ventilation openings when the exhaust fans are not running so CO_2 can't escape through your intake or exhaust vents. It's amazing how CO_2 can find its way out of even the smallest gaps.

Nutrient (or "Wet") Plan

How and how often you need to water or fertigate the plants in your garden is the next garden design challenge to tackle. Rarely, if ever, are water faucets or hose bibs right next to where the plants are located. Here are a few ideas for planning the movement of liquids through your grow space.

Water, Nutrients and Your Grow System

While we will explore grow systems in-depth in the next chapter, here we need to consider how those grow systems will be provided with the water and nutrient solutions they need and how any run off will be accommodated. Except for hand watering, every grow system needs a substantial amount of water and/or nutrients available, and many of them also require periodic draining.

That's a lot of heavy liquid to move around, enclose, pump and possibly dispose of, perfectly in balance with the needs of the garden and of course (ideally) without spilling a drop. Some grow systems contain the nutrient solution/water inside secure reservoirs or grow sites so there is little chance of the solution leaking out except when it's being actively handled. Deep water culture and ebb-and-flow systems are examples of this liquid management strategy.

Other grow systems constantly circulate or spray the nutrient solution; with these systems there is the opportunity for a leak to form and the solution to find its way out of the system. Nutrient film and aeroponic grow systems fall into this category. Obviously, more protection against leaks and sprays is needed for when using those types of grow systems.

Virtually all grow systems except hand watering utilize a reservoir from which they draw nutrients or water either on-demand or on a time schedule. How the reservoir is filled and drained if necessary are essential components of your nutrient/wet plan.

Moving Water

Women in Africa reportedly spend 25% of their time carrying water, which is a documented source of both physical disability and economic disadvantage. Do you want to become one of them? Assuming that answer is "no," then listen up: don't allow yourself to become a slave to carrying around heavy buckets of liquid. That is, if you value your time and your back.

Plan for the weight of water you'll need and how far you'll have to move it. Each gallon weighs 8.3 pounds, so it adds up quick: a full five-gallon bucket weighs more than 40 pounds. Worse, the buckets and reservoirs that we use are not ergonomically designed like weights at the gym. It's a lot harder to carry 40 pounds of water dangling at the end of one arm in a bucket, held by a flimsy metal bail, then it is to carry around a 40- or 50-pound dumbbell.

Regardless of how you feed your garden, from hand watering to recirculating setups, you may have to lug or pump both water and nutrients around. Consider these ways to lighten the load:

- If you have flexibility with respect to where your garden will be located, put it as close to your water source as possible.
- If you're building a grow box or adapting a closet, give yourself enough room to maneuver by building or choosing one with larger doors versus small ones.
- Consider putting the nutrient reservoir in a separate section of the grow facility, closet or grow box that's partitioned off and light-sealed, so you can change the nutrients at any time instead of waiting for when the lights are on.

With respect to your water source, if you filter your garden's water, reduce carrying distance by positioning the water filter as close to where you mix your nutrients as possible. Many growers choose to plumb reverse-osmosis (R/O) filters directly to the water supply. When permanently installing an R/O filter, consider investing in a leak detector so you can discover any leaks as soon as they happen and prevent any damage that might arise from the additional plumbing.

Home growers can attach small reverse-osmosis filters to many bathroom sinks by replacing the sink's screen or aeration fitting with a screw-in hose thread adapter. The small R/O system can then be used in the bathroom, with clean water collected directly into a nutrient mixing bucket and wastewater drained out via the sink or bathtub. This is a great option for renters, who can't make hard modifications to their homes.

Electrical Plan

The last major step in designing your grow space is an electrical plan that considers the physical layout of your grow space, how many lights you need, where and how they will be mounted, how you plan to control the environment, and how you'll water/feed the plants as all of these garden attributes may require electrical power.

Here are a few tips for putting together a safe and effective electrical installation in your grow space. These are only tips: if you're building out a commercial grow facility, please be sure to work with a competent professional electrician!

Power Placement

How much electrical power do you need? How many outlets do you need? Where should they be positioned? Can you move them if necessary?

Start your power plan by computing the total amount of electricity you'll need for your garden. For each electrical device you're planning to use, such as fans, pumps, timers, and so forth, look up the power requirements, which may be listed on the device's label, in the manufacturer's documentation, or online.

If you can't locate the power requirements for a device, use a "Kill-A-Watt" meter, or similar device, to measure the device's electrical demand. Even if you can find a device's power consumption, it's a good idea to confirm the actual wattage with a meter. Kill-A-Watt meters are inexpensive, and by using one you'll learn quite a bit about your actual power usage–some of it might surprise you.

Keeping in mind our earlier conversation about in-rush current, you need to plan your electrical system around the device's highest electrical demand value, not its lowest. Consider what happens in the event of a power outage. When the power comes back on, all the devices will turn on at the same time, drawing their highest electrical consumption all at the same time–which might be enough to trip a breaker and turn everything back off.

The 80% Load Rule

The 80% load rule says never exceed 80% capacity of any electrical circuit. How do you know whether you're overloading an electrical circuit? Use V = I x R, which states: voltage (V, measured in volts) equals impedance (I, measured in amps) times resistance (R, measured in watts).

$$V \text{ (volts)} = I \text{ (amps)} \times R \text{ (watts)}$$

Electrical circuits are wired to support a certain number of amps, usually 15 or 20. Add up the amps consumed by the equipment you plan to plug into each circuit that serves your grow space. For example, if your LED grow light uses 1000 watts of 120 volt power, how many amps is it using?

We need to rearrange the equation from the previous page and solve like this:

$$I \text{ (amps)} = R \text{ (watts)} / V \text{ (volts)}$$
$$I = 1000 \text{ watts} / 120 \text{ volts}$$
$$\text{Current draw for this light} = 8.33 \text{ amps}$$

If the anticipated load on any circuit is 80% or more of its rated capacity, some of the equipment must be moved to another circuit. Overloaded circuits generate excess heat and can start fires. In the example above only one 1000 watt grow light can be used on a 15 amp circuit. It would require a 20 amp circuit to power two 1000 watt grow lights and nothing else on it.

When planning your garden's electrical system:

- Verify the capacity and voltage of the outlets in the grow space. Are they 120 or 240 volt? 15 or 20 amp circuits? A simple way to do this is to head out to the circuit breaker panel and find the circuit that runs into the grow space. This can be accomplished easily with the aid of a "circuit tracer". The amperage is noted on the individual breaker for that electrical circuit. 120 versus 240 volts should be obvious based on the plug type in the wall. The standard two-vertical-slot outlet is 120 volts. 240 volt outlets come in a lot of varieties, are often round, and generally include at least one diagonally positioned slot. If you're not comfortable doing this kind of investigation, call an electrician. He or she can tell you what you need to know.
- Never load a circuit with equipment that draws more than 80% of its amp rating.
- Run upper and lower plug strips in small grow spaces to ensure short, clean electrical runs. Nothing is worse than fighting electrical cords when trying to fix something.

120 vs. 240 Volts

The difference between 120 and 240 volts often confuses people. From an electrical rate standpoint, the cost is the same–2.5 amps of 120 volts is the same cost as 1.25 amps of 240 volts. All residential power in North America is provided to your electric panel as 240 volts. The wiring consists of two "hot" 120 volt "legs" and a neutral "leg". For a 120 volt circuit, one of the hot legs and the neutral are used. For a 240 volt circuit, both the hot legs and the neutral are used. So what's the difference? The amperage. 240 volt devices use half the amperage as 120 volt ones.

$$\text{Remember from before that watts/volts} = \text{amps}$$
$$1000 \text{ watts}/120 \text{ volts} = 8.33 \text{ amps}$$
$$1000 \text{ watts}/240 \text{ volts} = 4.16 \text{ amps}$$

Because 240 volt devices use lower amperage, they tend to operate cooler. Lower operating temperatures don't provide much value for LED gardeners–the lights don't emit as much heat as HIDs. For commercial gardeners who use a lot of 1000 watt ballasts, however, the heat savings can add up quickly.

Backup Power Supplies

Every indoor garden experiences a power outage from time to time. Plan for this inevitability so you can minimize its impact on your garden. These impacts vary widely based on garden size, crops grown, and the plants stage of growth. There are no secret formulas and few rules of thumb for handling a power outage. Here are some thoughts on getting through an outage:

Universal Power Supply (UPS)

UPS units provide backup electricity from minutes to hours depending on the size. Large UPS units can be quire costly, so this solution works best in smaller grow spaces. Make sure to do your homework on how much power a particular unit can supply before relying on it to save you. You need to know how much time you have before it runs out.

Backup Generator

"Firing up the genny" can restore power to larger grows, so long as there is a generator connection to the electric panel and a transfer switch. Generators provide power as long as a fuel source is available, so they are better for extended outages than UPS units. In areas with frequent power outages, consider installing an automatic backup generator plumbed to the facility's natural gas supply to ensure hassle-free continuous electricity.

Controller/Timer Batteries

Some environmental controllers and timers have batteries inside that keeps the settings when the power goes out. Replace these once a year to be safe. Be sure to check the time on all controllers and timers once the power is restored and adjust as necessary.

Cheap Timers and Controllers

Be warned: there are lots of cheaply built timers and controllers on the market, and these can create safety hazards. As with garden lights, there are plenty of manufacturers that make cheap knockoff copies of the leading garden controllers. Many of these products have not been safety tested and are imported from places where stringent safety regulations don't exist. You trust these controllers to maintain your garden's environment; don't cheap out and buy a substandard unit. Make sure any timer or environmental controller used in your garden comes from a reputable manufacturer and has a UL, CE, or ETL mark to ensure that it has been certified by a recognized testing agency.

 **Sloper Says**

If your timers or environmental controllers have user-changeable fuses, make sure to check them after every grow cycle and replace them yearly. I once had a controller fail and almost wipe out my garden over a 25-cent fuse.

Even the minor failure of a timer or controller, such as it keeping inaccurate time or the failure of one of its functions, can reduce your harvest by creating out-of-spec conditions in your garden. A major failure such as an electrical short could cause a fire or a dangerous accumulation of CO_2. Keep away from junk–it costs you even more down the road when you have to replace it.

Care for Your Extension Cords

Extension cords need to be properly managed in order to be used safely in your garden. Did you know that dozens of US homes burn down each year due to extension cords that overheated because they were left in a tightly coiled pile?

A pile or coil of powered electrical cord generates heat as the electricity spins around and around inside it. The cord can get hot enough to catch anything combustible near it on fire. To reduce this hazard, use extension cords that are the correct length whenever possible.

A visit to an electronic specialty store should yield short, one-to-two-foot extension cords handy for connecting various equipment to timers and plug strips. If an appropriate length of extension cord is not available, make sure any excess length lies flat, is out of the way, and is not bunched or tightly coiled. Consider tacking long extension cord runs to the wall to keep them straight and out of the way.

When you're not using an extension cord, make sure it's properly stored. Don't coil or fold it tightly–the kinks this creates will prevent it from lying flat on next use. Coil the cord loosely and put it away flat. Putting your unused cords away with care ensures they will perform for you in the future. Also, clearly separating unused extension cords from those in use will prevent the mistake of plugging in a piled up or coiled extension cord or disconnecting a cord that is in use by mistake.

Use Drip Loops

Drip loops are a common electrical safety practice; they're nothing magical but can save you a call to the electrician. A drip loop is a deliberately created low point in the electrical cord that runs between a piece of electrical equipment and the electric socket. The low point allows any water that might accidently travel along the cord to drip off before entering the socket.

For example, go outside and look up at where the electrical main enters your house or building. Notice how the wires dip down before rising up to enter the conduit that goes into the structure. Those are drip loops. A drip loop should be used whenever an electrical device is in or near a water source. If you can, clip the low point in the cord to the wall to ensure that it stays below the outlet.

Security

One topic that's critical to consider when planning your grow space is security: how will you prevent unauthorized access to your garden?

For the hobbyists, security is typically a locked entrance. A locked door prevents someone from unintentionally breaking the dark cycle by opening the door at the wrong time, contaminating your garden with pests or fungus, inadvertently messing with temperature and humidity levels, or letting the CO_2 out (if you're enriching CO_2). You're trying to emulate Mother Nature in your grow space, which is hard enough to do without the door swinging open all the time and upsetting the delicate balance that you work so hard to maintain.

 Zen Gardening

Did you know that many garden pests hitchhike on gardeners' clothes, shoes, or hands? Keeping visitors out of the garden helps to keep pests in check, as does washing your hands, wearing clean clothes, and sanitizing shoes (if entering a walk-in grow space or commercial grow).

Modern commercial grow facilities have serious security. Armed guards, bullet proof glass and walls, man traps and alarmed doors are a few of the security measures that need to be cleared prior to entering the main areas of the facility. Everyone who visits needs to have photo identification. A log–electronic or on paper– is generally kept of everyone entering and leaving the facility. Badged access is required to different sections of the facility, staff and visitors often have to pass through several secured doors before entering an individual flower room. And if that's not enough, every inch of the facility is on camera and every action is recorded.

Commercial grow facilities with strict pest management programs require visitors to "suit up" before entering. This requires donning a Tyvek (or similar) suit, wearing disposable gloves and hair/beard nets. The final step is to spend 15-30 seconds in an air shower to remove contaminants prior to entering.

Hobby Grow Space Options

Hobbyists can let their imaginations wander when it comes to finding a place for your LED grow room. This section explores grow space options available to hobbyists, but not commercial growers, per se. The commercial guys may consider using some of these grow space options for test grows, but in general their grow space options begin with the build-out of a commercial space.

The great news for small growers is that LED grow lights allow you to grow in so many more spaces than you can with other garden lights, because they run cooler and require less bulky companion equipment– particularly smaller filters and ventilation fans. Once your garden is up and running, you'll likely find yourself looking around your friend's homes and thinking, "Hmmm… I could grow in that space, and that space, and that space…"

The two most basic options for a small indoor grow space are a prebuilt structure such as a closet or bedroom, or a temporary or freestanding space such as a grow tent or a homebuilt grow box–either a converted piece of furniture such as a wardrobe or storage cabinet or something built from scratch. Regardless of the space you choose, make sure the roof of the structure is strong. LED grow lights are heavy, as are fans and filters which are often mounted at the top of the grow space.

Closet/Whole Room

Growing in a closet or in an entire room can be the easiest way to go because the structure is already built for you. The biggest challenge to growing in these gardens is finding a secure method to hang the lights, fans, and filters. The plaster ceilings in most houses were not designed to support very much weight. Make sure that you attach your lights and other ceiling-mounted equipment to the ceiling rafters or to brackets or a frame that is connected to the rafters.

 **Zen Gardening**

When planning the location of the garden, consider the natural temperature variations within your house or apartment. In the northern hemisphere, the northern-most rooms in the house are generally a few degrees cooler than the southern parts of the home.

You also need to block out all unwanted light sources such windows and/or door jams, sealing them completely so there are no light leaks during your garden's dark cycle. Next, add ventilation—both fresh air coming in and garden air going out. In a full room, adding air intake and exhaust vents can be tricky and lead to an unattractive result, such as installing a vent in the hallway or the closet door. Some people cut a board to fit into the window, bolt on an HVAC duct flange, and then use an air duct to run their exhaust out the window. Neither of these two options is aesthetically pleasing, and they can also tip off the location of your indoor garden (an important consideration if you're trying to keep your garden in "stealth mode").

The most effective way to provide intake and exhaust ventilation in a whole room or built-in closet is to take advantage of adjacent air spaces. Instead of installing darkroom louver vents in a door, take a look inside the closets. A common design element in suburban American homes is a built-in closet that is essentially a big empty box between bedrooms with an interior partition, and doors on either side facing into the two rooms. If a closet in your grow room shares a wall with a closet in the next room, consider drawing cool air in from the other room through darkroom louver vents installed in the wall between the two closets. Leave the closet doors open on both sides to ensure adequate air flow and push the clothes in the closets out of the way of the vents.

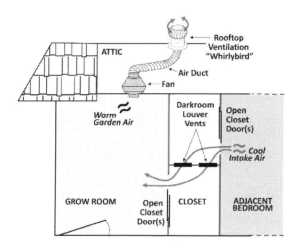

Regardless of your intake air source, it's important to exhaust the spent, heated air from your grow room out and away from your plants. If your grow room is in a one-story house or the upper floor of a multi-story home, consider cutting a hole through the ceiling of the room or closet into the home's attic space and then hanging your exhaust fan near this hole and pushing the hot air out through an air duct that extends through the attic to a rooftop ventilation "whirlybird". If your home already has an active attic exhaust system, you may be able to get away with simply exhausting into the attic.

Closet/Whole Room Pros:

- Simple, as most of the structure build out is already completed for you
- When done right, these grow rooms can be very stealthy
- Easy to secure by adding a lock(s)
- Easy to customize to your personal gardening style

Closet/Whole Room Cons:

- Light leaks can be tough to seal, particularly at the entrance
- May not be worth the physical modifications if renting

Grow Tents

Grow tents grows are perfect for temporary gardens or renters. They are available in many different sizes and shapes and can be set up and taken down quickly. There are many high-quality grow tents available as well as cheap knockoffs–be warned.

Before buying any tent, go see one for yourself at a local indoor gardening center. Does it look solidly constructed? Give it a shake test–how does it feel? Make sure the roof is capable of holding lots of weight or can be easily reinforced to hold more weight. Cheaper grow tents sometimes skimp on upper crossbeams, which limits the amount of weight they will support, while some premium models have snap-in reinforcements strong enough to hold a heavy light, carbon filter and a fan. Some tent manufacturers also offer snap-in equipment panels, handy for keeping timers, controllers, and fans in easy reach and protected from fluid leaks by being raised off the floor.

 SAFETY FIRST

Some of the early grow tents were manufactured with PVC sheeting. When PVC heats up, it releases dioxin, which is toxic to plants and humans. Some of these early grow tents actually poisoned the gardens they were supposed to protect. PVC has been phased out of most grow tents; make sure to check before buying.

Heavy-duty zippers are a must as they will be opened and closed often. Most grow tents also feature gussets near the top and bottom for ventilation ducts and for electrical cords that run into and out of the tent. Make sure any tent you're considering has at least one of these gussets at both top and bottom and that you can completely close them to prevent light leaks.

Speaking of light leaks, before you buy a tent, stand inside it and ask the shop clerk to completely close the tent and seal all of its openings. Look to see whether any light leaks into the inside–most grow tents are not completely light tight. If the tent leaks light, should set it up in a room stays dark during your garden's dark period.

Some grow tents feature Velcro-closed observation windows so you can take a peek inside without disturbing the garden's environment. These can be handy for quick garden checks–as long as the observation windows do not cause light leaks and you don't open them during the garden's dark period.

Since they are tents, the walls have a tendency to be sucked inward when there is too much back pressure. One way to solve this problem is to have similarly sized intake and exhaust fans. You will want the exhaust fan to be slightly stronger than the intake to create the slightest back pressure–but not too much.

If your design allows for only one fan, consider reinforcing the walls with pegboard to make them more rigid. It's very easy to cut and can be installed with zip ties: use it on three sides but leave the font side you use to access your garden as-is.

Grow Tent Pros:

- Easy to set up–holes, flaps, and gussets in the correct places
- Designed specifically by gardeners for gardeners
- Extremely portable and reusable

Grow Tent Cons:

- Potential back pressure issues
- May not be completely lightproof; may need to use in a darkened room

Grow Boxes

A grow box is a portable grow space that can be moved–either as a self-contained unit with wheels or as an enclosure that can be assembled and disassembled as needed. Grow boxes differ from grow tents as they are solid structures, can be secured with locks, and can be made to be "stealthy". Many grow boxes are homemade, and there are also several companies building grow boxes ranging in size from a countertop appliance to full-sized shipping containers.

Homebuilt grow boxes are the most fun of all indoor grow spaces. They can be 100% custom-built; your imagination, skills, and tools are your only limits. Homebuilt grow boxes can be created in any shape or size your situation allows.

 **Sloper Says**

Note of caution: building grow boxes can be addictive. Build one and more will follow!

Almost anything can be converted into a grow box. The smallest of gardens can grow inside a desktop computer case, while large gardens can occupy a wardrobe cabinet or armoire. Old refrigerators and storage cabinets can be converted to gardens–assuming you have the skills and the patience to complete the conversion (including properly handling and disposing of toxic substances you might encounter, such as refrigerant).

Need a quick grow box? Foam insulation board, aka "foam core," plus good old-fashioned duct tape could be your answer. Foam core is sold in home and hardware stores in 4'x8' sheets in several thicknesses. Tape four walls together, tape on a ceiling, and cut in a door and vents, and you've got a grow box. Buy a stand or build one from 2x4s to hang your light, fan, and filter, and you're ready to grow. Stand the grow box on a tarp or plastic sheet to catch any spills. Foam core grow boxes are a great temporary solution and can be quickly cut down and stuffed into trash bags for disposal.

Grow Box Pros:

- You can build a grow space and environment that is custom-tailored to exactly meet your needs, growing style, and constraints
- You can get very clever in configuring your garden, particularly the locations of the air vent and the electrical connections
- They are so much fun to build–you get to build the better mousetrap

- Your garden will recognize and reward your effort

Grow Box Cons:

- They can require lots of tools
- They are time consuming to build

8: Grow Systems

While we touched on grow systems in the last chapter, it's a big topic that deserves more discussion. There are lots of choices: hydroponic, aeroponic, active, passive, recirculating, run to waste... If you ask five gardeners which growing system is best, you're likely to get seven to ten answers.

When choosing a growing system, go with what works for you and not what is "supposed" to be the best according to some "expert". Before plunking down your hard-earned cash for a growing system read this chapter carefully then review the growing systems comparison chart at the end.

Every growing system has its pros and cons that present tradeoffs all gardeners must resolve for themselves. Some systems are easy to set up and take down but hard to clean or use lots of nutrients. Some systems require electrical power. Some systems use media that can be cleaned and reused instead of thrown out at the end of a run, which may be important for apartment dwellers with limited trash-disposal capacity or commercial growers looking to reduce costs or their waste stream.

Talk to other gardeners about their experiences with different growing systems, if you can. Whatever system you choose, stick with it for several harvests until you fully understand how it works and how to "dial it in" for your particular growing style. In your quest to become Mother Nature, lots of things get thrown at you in the beginning. Take your time and learn. If you make changes too fast, you might miss what you should be learning about gardening instead of just learning how to manage a gardening system.

Growing System Elements

Growing systems are classified by how the nutrient solution is fed to the plants. Some systems use the solution only once; these are called "run to waste" systems. Others reuse the solution for multiple feedings; these are called "recirculating" systems. Run-to-waste and recirculating growing systems can be "active" or "passive".

Active vs. Passive

The main difference between active and passive growing systems is that active systems need electricity to power water pumps that deliver the nutrient solution to the plants through feed lines, sprayers, or channels. Passive systems don't require electricity, relying on capillary action and/or gravity to deliver the nutrient solution.

Run to Waste

Hand watering a houseplant is the most basic form of run-to-waste irrigation. Greenhouse tomato producers often run to waste: their tomatoes are grown on the ground in pots or grow bags and watered from the top, with excess nutrients running directly into the ground. Run-to-waste watering can be used with just about any grow media.

The "waste" nutrients can be removed from the garden in many ways, including catching them in a plastic tray under a pot, a second "catch" reservoir, or a drain hose running out of the grow space. Be sure to responsibly dispose of your waste nutrients when using the run-to-waste method. Feed the nutrient runoff to bushes in your backyard, or dilute and spray it onto your lawn: this solution contains high-quality, bioavailable nutrients that the plants around you would eat like candy. Don't toss waste nutrients down the drain if there is any alternative; see the "Salt Neutral" section in the next chapter for details on why this is a poor practice.

Recirculating

Recirculating systems pump the nutrient solution from a reservoir to the plants and then collect the runoff back into the reservoir to be fed to the plants again. These systems are extremely popular with indoor gardeners because they contain the runoff and are only drained periodically–great for indoor hobby grow spaces where drainage may not be readily available.

Recirculating systems are typically used with hydroponic growing media, with the nutrient solution being used for a week before being changed out for fresh solution. As with run-to-waste systems, dispose of the nutrient solution on an outside garden instead of dumping it down the drain, if possible.

Grow Media Considerations

Except for the purely hydroponic growing systems (NFT, aeroponic, and DWC), you'll need to choose a growing media. There are many things to consider: simplicity, environmental friendliness, cleanliness, weight, and cation-exchange capacity.

Also think about where your garden is situated and how you will dispose of used grow media. If your grow space is upstairs or multi-level, you might want to select a lightweight media such as rockwool instead of heavy grow rocks. If you want to grow in soil, where will you dispose of used soil? Recycling indoor garden soil into outdoor beds is an environmentally friendly choice so long as you screen out and dispose of any perlite in the mix. Perlite, a white, lightweight material made from volcanic rock, will rise to the top of the beds when watered, where it will be blown around your yard by the wind.

Cation-exchange capacity (CEC) measures how well a grow media retains or "binds" elemental minerals contained in the nutrients you feed the plants. Growing media with higher CEC will be able to feed the plants longer than media with low CEC.

Naturally derived growing media, including shredded coconut husks ("coco coir") and peat have relatively high CEC, in contrast with manmade media such as rockwool cubes and grow rocks that provide little if any CEC. When using a media with high CEC, be sure to watch the plants carefully to look for signs of over- or under-feeding and adjust accordingly.

Media Type	Pros	Cons	CEC
Soilless Mixes	Reusable, can be pre-charged with nutrients, good for beneficial microorganisms	Heavy to carry, can be over watered, messy	Low to High
Coco Coir	Reusable, environmentally friendly, great for beneficial organisms	Heavy to carry, messy	Medium
Rockwool	Simple to use, lightweight	Not environmentally friendly, needs conditioning	None
Expanded Clay Pellets	Great aeration, reusable	Heavy to carry, messy, needs to be prewashed	Little to None
Perlite	Lightweight, great for "lightening" up soilless mixes	Messy, dust is an inhalation hazard	None

It's not always obvious whether a particular growing media has a high or low cation exchange capacity. If you're not 100% certain about the CEC value of a grow media, ask your garden supplier for details. Pick one media to start with and stick with it for your first few harvests. Remember: in the beginning, gardening is all about learning, so go slow with changes. If you're new to growing indoors, start out with a high-quality soilless mix.

Soil vs. Soilless

One of my larger pet peeves is the misuse of the term "soil" in indoor gardening. The base components of soil are sand, silt and clay. The ratio between these three ingredients will dictate whether it's a sandy, loamy or clay soil. Go check a bag of indoor grow mix—does it have these three ingredients in it? Likely, *no*.

Most potting and planting mixes are actually considered soilless grow mixes. They typically have a base of coco coir or sphagnum, commonly called peat moss, perlite for aeration, and enrichments such as earth worm castings, beneficial microbes or other additives. Soilless growing mixes can either be pre-charged with plant nutrients or not, leaving the grower in charge of feeding.

Growing System Types

Growing systems are primarily categorized by how they provide irrigation/fertigation to the plants. Different types of grow systems also offer different operating characteristics, such as how often they need to be tended, whether the plants can be easily rearranged, and their level of stability/risk of failure.

Hand Watering

Hand watering is the simplest form of a grow system. I think everyone knows what hand watering is, I'm just including it to be complete. The only problem with it is you have to remember to water! I tease about that but you wouldn't believe how many "black-thumb" gardeners simply forget to water. I personally I call them "black-brainers"!

Hand Watering Pros:
- Grower has complete control over individual plant needs
- Least expensive option

Hand Watering Cons:
- May require daily watering
- You're carrying water

Subirrigation

Subirrigation is the process where water and nutrients are delivered below the surface of the grow media and absorbed upwards through passive wicking. This method can be very easy to set up and operate.

 **Sloper Says**

Never leave your plants sitting in water–the level MUST rise and fall. Plants can drown and you also run the risk of root rot.

Subirrigation systems fall into two different types–gravity-fed and wick based. Gravity-fed systems position the reservoir above the plants, with tubing to carry the nutrient solution down to the plants utilizing a valve to regulate wet and dry cycles. Wick based grow systems passively feed the garden by capillary action: the nutrient solution moves along a cloth or rope "wick" that runs from the reservoir below to the plants above keeping the growing media moist.

One of the best applications of subirrigation I've seen used a baby pool filled with nutrient solution, with a crate set in it to support the plants. Wicks made from rope were run through the bottom of each pot before it was filled with potting mix and planted. The plants were then positioned on the crate with the ropes hanging into the baby pool, so that the nutrient solution could wick up through capillary action to moisten the pots.

Commercial subirrigation systems, found in garden centers and hardware store garden sections, utilize wicking mats that provide moisture/nutrients to the base of potted plants on racks or trays. This method of watering cuts down wasted water, labor costs and reduces the potential pest and fungal problems associated with top watering.

Subirrigation is my preferred method for hobbyists growing indoors. Not only does it allow for simple but complete watering and feeding, it does so without getting the surface of the grow media wet. This alone cuts down on pests such as white flies and gnats. With dry conditions on the surface, fungus and molds don't grow well either.

Subirrigation Pros:
- Simple
- Cuts pest problems down

Subirrigation Cons:
- Roots don't grow in the top layer of the grow media

Ebb-and-Flow

Ebb-and-flow systems, also known as "flood and drain," periodically immerse plant roots in nutrient solution by pumping the solution either into a shallow tray in which the plants sit, or into individual plant grow buckets. Tray-style ebb-and-flow systems consist of a formed plastic or fiberglass tray plus a reservoir, usually positioned beneath the tray. Plants are generally grown in rockwool cubes in this type of growing system.

When it's time to feed the plants, a water pump in the reservoir is turned on and pumps the nutrient solution up into to tray through an inlet tube connected to the tray at its lowest point. The tray fills up to a defined depth, determined by a second pipe called the "overflow tube" that's a few inches taller than the inlet pipe. When the solution's depth exceeds the height of the overflow tube, the solution flows back down into the reservoir through the overflow tube, thus maintaining a constant depth in the tray.

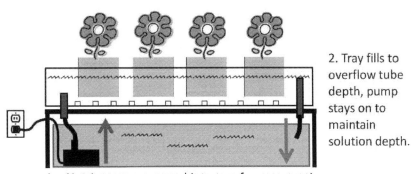

2. Tray fills to overflow tube depth, pump stays on to maintain solution depth.

1. Nutrients are pumped into tray from reservoir.
3. When pump shuts off, nutrients drain back into reservoir through pump.

The pump stays on long enough to allow the solution to fill the grow tray and fully saturate the growing media. Then the pump is turned off, and the nutrient solution drains back into the reservoir though the pump. As the nutrient solution drains out of the tray or buckets, it also pulls air down into the plants' root zones and provides oxygen to the roots. A simple household timer or an elaborate controller can be used to control the flood cycle.

A barrel-and-bucket ebb-and-flow system operates similarly but uses a large barrel for the reservoir and individual grow buckets instead of a tray. A controller unit stands in between the barrel and the buckets and controls both the depth of the nutrient solution flood and its timing. These systems can be configured in just about any size and shape to fit your growing needs, and more grow pots can be added at any time, up to the capacity of the reservoir barrel.

At the start of the feed, the controller activates a pump in the reservoir that starts filling the controller bucket to a specified depth. Since the grow pots are all plumbed to the controller unit and water "seeks its own level," the liquid level in all of the pots will even out to the level in the controller unit. When the pots are full, the reservoir pump is turned off and the nutrient solution is left to stand in the buckets for a few minutes. At the end of the feed cycle, a pump in the controller unit pumps all of the water back into the reservoir. Then the controller unit waits for the next feed cycle.

Grow buckets in this type of growing system consist of two plastic pots nested inside each other. The grow media and plant sit in the upper pot, which has holes in the bottom to allow the nutrient solution to saturate the media and root zone. The lower pot is plumbod to the controller. Two-part buckets allow the gardener to rotate the plants by moving the upper pots around to even out light exposure, though this should be done infrequently and carefully to avoid damaging the plants.

One of the big advantages of ebb-and-flow growing systems is that they are extremely reliable: Each pump is on for a few minutes per cycle so your exposure to pump failure is small. There is one way to eliminate this risk altogether in small gardens: as long as the gardener has a few minutes every day to manually feed the garden, a high/low bucket system can replace the pump with gravity and some heavy lifting.

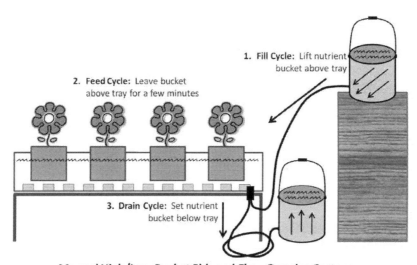

Manual High/Low Bucket Ebb and Flow Growing System

With the high/low bucket system, the nutrient solution is mixed in a bucket (five gallons or less, unless you want to hurt your back) that has a hole drilled near the bottom with a flexible hose attached that's connected to the drain hole of an ebb-and-flow tray. The bucket is set on the floor near the tray.

When it's time to feed the plants, the bucket is hung or set above the level of the tray. Gravity will drain the nutrient solution into the tray. The bucket stays in this position for a few minutes to allow the nutrient solution to saturate the growing media, then the bucket is set back down on the floor so that the nutrient solution can drain back into it. This cycle is repeated as necessary depending on plant needs and grow media.

Ebb-and-Flow Pros:
- Easy to set up and move plants
- Extremely reliable: no thin drip lines to clog
- Forces an "air exchango" in the root zone

Ebb-and-Flow Cons:
- Uses more nutrients than other systems
- A larger pump may be needed than for other growing systems

Drip Irrigation

Drip systems are very similar to ebb and flow, but instead of filling the whole tray with nutrient solution, each plant is watered from the top via a drip line or drip ring. While drip systems typically collect the runoff to recirculate, they also come in run-to-waste models. Drip systems are appropriate for any type of grow media.

Since the nutrient solution is delivered directly to each plant, drip systems use nutrients very efficiently. They are trickier to set up: each plant needs one or more drip lines and/or drip rings, which if positioned improperly can lead to under- or over-watering. Clogged lines are also a risk. A clog in an individual drip line can kill a plant if not caught in time, and a clog in the main feed line can kill the whole garden. Plus, all of those drip lines are in the way if the plants need to be rotated or separated.

Drip irrigation run to waste is the most common type of irrigation I see in commercial grow facilities. Make sure to sanitize the lines after each grow cycle. This can be accomplished by pumping a hydrogen peroxide solution through the drip lines. Use caution as concentrated hydrogen peroxide is an oxidizer. Use proper personal protection when handling it.

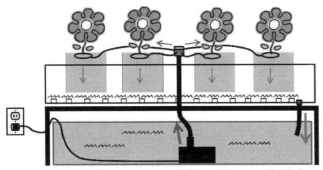

2. Nutrients drip through growing media, then drain into the tray.

1. Nutrients are pumped through a manifold that distributes the solution to plants via drip lines.

Drip Pros:
- Efficient use of nutrients
- Drip nozzle flow rates can be customized to the needs of individual plants

Drip Cons:
- More complex setup with one or more drip lines to each plant
- Drip lines can clog
- Difficult to rearrange plants

Nutrient Film Technique or "NFT"

NFT systems suspend plants in small plastic baskets commonly called "net pots" above a channel in which a low-volume trickle of nutrient solution constantly flows across their bare roots. In the ideal NFT system, the water level is very thin, hence the name nutrient "film". The plants' roots grow into a thick mat in the channel, with the bottom of the mat laying in the nutrient film and the top moist but exposed to air. NFT systems, properly used, provide an optimal balance of water, nutrients, and oxygen to the plants, accelerating growth and promoting heavy harvests.

Because NFT systems do not use growing media such as soil or rockwool, they are highly sensitive to interruptions. Growing media provides a great buffer for plants: it keeps roots moist between feedings, can absorb and release nutrients when the plant needs them, and retains oxygen in the root zone.

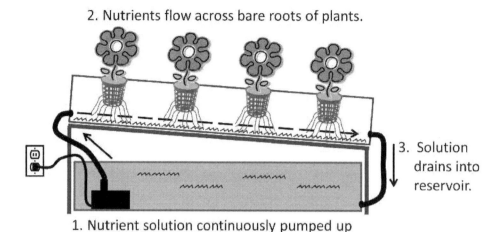

2. Nutrients flow across bare roots of plants.

3. Solution drains into reservoir.

1. Nutrient solution continuously pumped up into NFT channel from reservoir.

Without growing media to protect them, NFT-grown plants can quickly dry out if the film is interrupted for any reason–a power outage, failed pump, or clogged line can kill an NFT garden in less than a day if not discovered right away. Consider using an UPS or backup generator if you grow in an area where power outages are common.

Nutrient Film Technique Pros:
- No grow media expense
- Efficient use of nutrients
- Superior plan growth due to high oxygen levels

Nutrient Film Technique Cons:
- Crop fails quickly if the pump fails
- You need to have a replacement pump on hand and check your garden frequently

Aeroponics or "Aero"

Similar to NFT, aeroponics is a growing method that exposes the bare roots of plants to nutrient solution and air. In this case, the roots hang in a chamber in which nutrient solution is either sprayed directly onto the roots or misted into the air surrounding the roots.

EXPERT CORNER

Consider cycling your Aero and NFT for a 5-10 seconds on and 20-30 off when using a UPS. This will allow it to power the machines longer in the event of an outage. Some experimentation is required!

Aeroponics was developed in the 1940s as a method to study plant root development. Aero differs from NFT in that the roots are contained with a large area versus a channel, and they are not necessarily constantly exposed to the nutrient solution. The plants consume nutrients from solution droplets that land on their roots, and the humid environment in the root chamber prevents the roots from drying out.

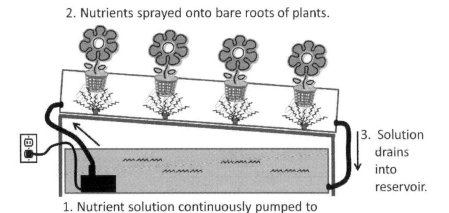

2. Nutrients sprayed onto bare roots of plants.

3. Solution drains into reservoir.

1. Nutrient solution continuously pumped to sprayers from the reservoir.

Many commercially produced cloning machines use aeroponic techniques to root cuttings. Aero systems are also available for full-sized plants, though they command a smaller share of the market than other types of growing systems. This is because, like NFT, aeroponic systems are more susceptible to failure–a power outage or pump failure can instantly leave the garden high and dry. Again, consider using an uninterrupted power supply (UPS) or backup generator if you live in an area where power outages are common.

Aeroponic Pros:
- No grow media expense
- Efficient use of nutrients
- Superior plant growth due to high oxygen levels

Aeroponic Cons:
- Crop fails quickly if the pump fails
- You need to have a replacement pump on hand and check your garden frequently

Deep Water Culture or "DWC"

DWC is a growing method in which the plants' bare roots are immersed in a solution of highly oxygenated, nutrient-rich water. The plants are suspended in the solution using plastic net pots or something similar depending on the manufacturer. Air is pumped into the DWC reservoir though air pumps and stones, earning this technique the alternate moniker "bubbleponics". DWC systems are often homemade setups that include a five-gallon bucket, a bucket lid with attached net pot, an air pump, and an air stone. Commercially produced systems are available in a large variety of configurations.

Deep water culture is a misnomer since the nutrient solution can actually be shallow or deep in these systems. "Direct water culture" would be better, since the root zone is completely immersed in the nutrient solution.

DWC systems are simple to set up and operate. Systems that use individual buckets allow plants to easily be rotated or moved to take best advantage of available light. DWC's downside is the risk of pump failure: if the air pump fails and the bubbles stop, the plant(s) can drown in a matter of hours. Garden checks are required several times a day.

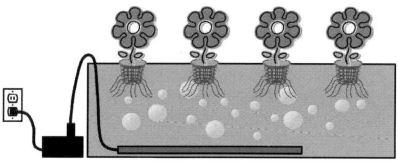

Plants are suspended in a nutrient solution reservoir
that is constantly aerated with an air pump and stone.

Like NFT and aeroponics, power failures can kill this type of garden. Again, consider using an uninterrupted UPS if you grow in an area where blackouts are common.

Deep Water Culture Pros:
- Great growth due to high oxygen levels
- Can be inexpensively made at home

Deep Water Culture Cons:
- Plant(s) can drown if the air pump fails
- May have problems with "thin air" at altitude
- You need to have a replacement pump on hand and check garden frequently

Growing System Gotchas

While setting up most growing systems is relatively simple, it's easy to get crossed up by one of these common goofs. Let's examine a few of the most common ones:

Water/Nutrient Leaks

Adding a leak detector to your garden equipment just in case something becomes backed up or spills is a good idea. It's easy to have a leak in your garden–with all of the hoses, fittings, reservoirs, and trays; it's inevitable that something will leak over time. Leak detectors range from simple units that sound an audible alarm to wireless sensors that call, text, or tweet to alert you of the flood. Let's be honest–it's a question of *when* not *if*… it's indoor gardening after all.

Also keep a wet/dry vacuum nearby to clean up spills. If you don't already have one, consider buying one of the vacuum heads designed to sit on a five-gallon bucket sold in hardware stores. They're inexpensive, and they're small enough to fit in all but the smallest of indoor gardens.

Kinked Tubing

Kinked hoses can spell disaster for an indoor garden. It's surprising how even a small bend in a hose can cause it to all but shut off flow. When it comes to tubing, like all critical equipment, "when in doubt, throw it out".

If the tubing that comes with a new growing system is kinked or if your tubing becomes kinked from poor storage or misuse, *replace it*. Don't be penny-wise and pound-foolish; tubing is cheap, and your garden is a labor of love.

Also, remember that "haste makes waste". If your growing system includes tubing, just assume it's kinked, and check it every chance you get. Be vigilant looking for telltale signs–drooping plants and light, dried-out containers. Whatever you do, don't let kinked tubing be your garden's downfall.

Odor Control

Let's face it: sometimes plant nutrients and the plants themselves stink. Good odor control can keep you on the good side of neighbors or family. Most indoor gardeners want a garden that does not draw attention to itself. Uncontrolled garden smells are an invitation for would-be intruders. It's very common for cities to require odor control in commercial facilities. Check your local laws.

 **Sloper Says**

I have a friend who was working on her garden just prior to going on vacation. Late for a flight, she quickly dropped the pump for her ebb-and-flow system into the reservoir without checking to be sure the hose was straight.

When she got home, she found the garden completely dried and fried: the tube that irrigated her tray had a pinch in it when it was purchased, creating a weak point that twisted just enough to almost completely block nutrient flow through the line. Fifty cents worth of new tubing when the system was set up, and/or a 10-second check when the pump was placed in the reservoir, would have saved the garden.

Ozone Generator

One method to clean up smells is to install an ozone generator. These machines move air over electrically charged plates to convert some of the oxygen (O_2) in the air into ozone (O_3). Ozone is a very reactive, unstable molecule. It wants to convert back to oxygen but must release energy before it can. Its energy is released when it reacts with organic matter such as odors and smoke particles as well as fungi and bacteria, giving ozone both odor control and cleansing characteristics.

Before you deploy an ozone generator, check to see how much ozone it produces which is measured in parts per million (PPM). Then verify that the ozone generator you want to use is legal where you want to use it, as some areas have banned ozone generators or have placed limits on allowed ozone concentrations output due to health concerns. Ozone can cause respiratory distress in sensitive people including asthma attacks and respiratory tract irritation.

Carbon Filter

A second method to remove garden smells is to use an activated carbon filter. Carbon is great at grabbing odors out of the air. During the activation process, carbon is heated to remove impurities and create an attractive space for odor particles. Other compounds such as zeolite are mixed in to increase the effectiveness of the filter. Carbon filters do have a useful life, check the label or ask the manufacturer and be ready to change them out down the road.

Speaking of filters, there's a longstanding debate about whether it's better to suck or blow contaminated air through a filter. Ask people their opinion and you'll hear both sides, with lengthy justifications. Make this decision based on your ventilation setup and where you have the room to set or mount your fan and filter.

The best argument for sucking though the filter is that you can use a pre-filter, which will extend the life of the filter itself.

While the fan/filter doesn't care too much about suck versus blow, the ducting does. Ducting works better when its being blown open instead of sucked through, which makes it want to close in due to back pressure, restricting air flow.

Configure your ventilation setup so you can get to the back of both the fan and filter, in case they need service or repairs. Also make sure there are as few sharp bends in your ventilation ducting as possible, which also adds back pressure.

9. How to Feed Plants

When it comes to feeding plants, it turns out that the "how" is just as important as the "what". It takes a lot to properly feed a garden: you need to determine how much nutrient solution your garden needs, how to make the solution as available to the plants as possible, how to identify nutrient deficiencies and excesses, and when beneficial microorganisms might be helpful.

We'll dig into the "what" to feed your garden in Chapter 10. In this chapter, you'll find ideas and information about the how's and why's of plant nutrition that you may have not seen or thought of before. Like this:

Feed Schedules–Don't Blindly Trust Them

Don't trust the "standard" feeding schedules printed on the back or side of bottles and boxes of nutrients designed for indoor growing. Ultimately the PPFD levels will dictate optimal nutrient strength. Lower light levels need lower nutritional strength and high light levels require higher nutritional strength.

Most of these feeding charts were developed for experienced gardeners who grow heavy-feeding plants under 1000 watt HID lamps. Almost everybody else will over/under feed their gardens if simply follow the manufacturers feed chart.

Adding to the problem, marketing campaigns for indoor garden nutrients are designed to make you believe that you need lots and lots of bottles. The companies that make and sell these products want you to think you need a multi-part base nutrient formula and a seemingly unlimited number of supplements or else your yields will suffer.

 Sloper Says

Many gardeners, searching for better results, keep trying out different nutrients thinking that they will find their "holy grail"–nutrients that allow their plants to thrive trouble-free.

But while searching for that Holy Grail, what did the gardener acquire? Experience. The health of any garden depends more on the gardener's experience than on the nutrients it was fed. With experience and your best "meter", your eyes, you will soon master indoor garden nutrition.

They might also tell you that your yields will *explode!* if you supplement with the latest bottle of plant go-go juice. Some supplements even promise results bordering on supernatural, such as vibrationally activated water that purportedly kills or prevents mildew or a spray that restores a plant's "natural genetic photosynthetic speed" to produce heavy harvests.

Stop listening to what the nutrient manufacturers say about what, how much, and how often to feed your garden, and start paying more attention to your plants. They will tell you how much they want to be fed. Nutrient manufacturers are in the business of selling bottles, more bottles, and even more bottles of plant food–not tending your garden. The more bottles you buy, the more money they make. Additionally make sure the feed chart matches the grow technique. Nutrient formulas for recirculating systems that change their nutrients weekly are typically stronger than for run to waste systems.

Feeding Your Plants: How Much?

With plant nutrition, less is usually more. Plants are much more in control of what they "eat" than we give them credit for: they've developed complex systems to attract the specific minerals they need and repel the ones they don't, primarily through root secretions. These secretions, also called "root extrudates", change conditions in the root zone, such as raising or lowering pH or changing the amount of carbohydrates in the grow media, which affects the composition of beneficial microorganisms in the grow media and also nutrient availability. Overfeeding can break down these regulatory processes.

All you really need to do is provide your garden with a wide range of the required nutrients, not too much and not too little, so the plants can pick and choose what they need in order to grow. Choose a good-quality nutrient designed to be used with your type of growing system and start by feeding your plants at about ¾ the suggested strength. Then keep a close eye on them.

 **Good Practice**

When watering plants in pots or containers, make sure you're really saturating the grow media. It's easy to pour some nutrient solution over a plant, see it quickly run out the bottom, and believe the job is done. Not necessarily.

The best way is to water a small amount, wait 3-4 minutes, water a bit more, wait 3-4 minutes, and then water the plant until saturated. The first two small waterings break the surface tension within the media and allow for full watering.

Is their green color getting lighter or darker? Lighter generally means the plant needs more nitrogen and possibly magnesium. Underfed plants may also develop weak stems and branches, grow slowly, or develop mildew. Any obvious problems should be treated directly (such as staking the plant or spraying for fungus), and the feeding solution should also be strengthened a bit. Continue to monitor and adjust until you find the feeding level at which the plants are lush and vigorously growing, able to stand on their own and absorb high levels of good-quality light.

A plant's nutritional needs may change over its life cycle, particularly with respect to potassium, one of the "big three" nutrients–nitrogen, phosphorous, and potassium. Many plants consume potassium in higher levels during their flowering and fruiting phases, which is why "bloom boost" supplements with high potassium levels are so popular. But with that popularity comes a problem: an overdose of phosphorus. We'll talk about this in greater detail in Chapter 10.

Overfeeding is worse than underfeeding, because it's harder to correct. You may be able to flush away some of the excess nutrients in a hydroponic system, but your garden might be stuck with the excess bound up in high CEC media. Flushing is discussed later in this chapter.

LEDs and Nutrition Levels

You may have heard that nutrient levels should be lower for LED-lit gardens versus gardens with other lights. In the early days, LED gardeners did generally feed ¼- to ½-strength solutions. This worked because older LED lights didn't have much power or produce much heat. Lower light and lower heat slows growth and lowers nutritional needs. After reading chapter 3, you now know why–RuBisCO needs proper temperatures to function properly.

The newer generation of LED grow lights, with higher light output, grow large plants with nutritional profiles similar to plants grown under any other indoor garden light. Ignore any advice you may find online or elsewhere about feeding LED gardens weak nutrient solutions. Plants grown under newer LED grow lights may even need *more* nutrition than their HID counterparts–it would be hard to say for sure without formal trials in a laboratory setting.

Foliar Feeding

Foliar feeding is another area where I have changed my mind. This practice needs some real scientific experimentation. Foliar feeding involves spraying a diluted nutrient solution directly onto the leaves. The conventional wisdom states that plants can absorb nutrients through their leaves.

Although once I promoted this concept, I'm not sure how effective it is anymore. All plants originally evolved outside and survive rainstorms. They have developed waxy coatings to keep water (and any contaminants in it) out. Foliar feeding might produce results on some plants but I am not sure it works universally. I am beginning to believe any apparent results may come from the nutrients that drip off the leaves to the soil and then are absorbed by the roots.

Recently someone presented alternative view to me about foliar feeding. His point was if Monsanto can get Roundup to kill plants where must be a way in though the leaves. It might have something to do a particular surfactant or other chemistry, but we all know it works. Again this is another area of needed cannabis specific research.

pH and Nutrient Availability

The **potential of hydrogen (pH)** of the nutrient solution you feed your plants, how acidic or basic, matters somewhat–but far less than many gardeners think. A pH of 7.0 is defined as neutral: solutions below that are acidic and above that are basic.

If your nutrient solution is way out of the normal range, either too acidic or basic, your plants will have a more difficult time absorbing the nutrients they need. Fortunately, most plants tolerate a wide range of pH values: for most, a pH between the low 5s and high 6s is fine for plants we typically grow indoors.

Adjusting the pH of your nutrients is very simple. If the pH is too low (5 or less), add pH up solution (a base). If the pH is too high, (7 or more) add pH down (an acid). Both pH up and pH down solutions are available at any indoor gardening store.

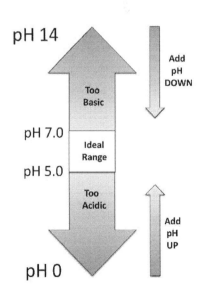

Indoor gardeners tend to stress about pH levels, mostly because they've been trained to. Nutrient manufacturers, hydro shop staff, and indoor gardening magazines all warn indoor gardeners on a regular basis that without proper pH levels, your plants will not be able to take up the nutrients they need, and the garden will suffer. Thus, at the first sign of a problem, many rookie gardeners blame out-of-spec pH. After all, since they followed the instructions on their nutrient bottles exactly, the problem must not be their fault. It must be due to pH swings causing nutritional lockouts.

🧑 Sloper Says

I once fed plants grown in a soilless mix a nutrient solution that was very acidic–pH below 4–for its entire life cycle due to a pH meter problem. I knew from looking at the garden that there was a problem, but I didn't suspect pH as the cause, because I assumed the meter was working fine. It appeared to calibrate properly.

Fortunately, the crop was growing in a high-quality soilless mix with lots of beneficial microorganisms added to the mix. The soil was able to buffer the negative effect of pH, so while this grow did not produce the best yield, it still produced a harvest.

There are growers who believe that changing the pH by 0.1 of a point a week during flowering, for example, 5.8–5.9–6.0–6.1 6.2... will improve harvest quality. While these gardeners swear this practice makes a difference, fine-tuning pH to this degree is completely unnecessary. There is simply no reason to be a slave to your garden to such an extreme.

Other growers swear there is a single perfect pH. I've come to realize the reason for "pH passion". pH meters have always been the least expensive meter used in a grow and pH is easy to alter. Since pH easily can be measured and "corrected" it's often blamed by thoughtless growers, vs. lighting issues which requires an expensive meter to measure. My advice: focus more on the environment and lighting and less on pH.

The most knowledgeable indoor gardeners skip the pH adjustment process entirely and still have amazing results with cannabis. Do your own experimenting and find what works in your garden. You just may find yourself leaving the pH meter on the shelf!

Personally I have not used a pH meter for well over a decade. Regardless of the grow style, from DWC to charged soilless mixes and everything in between, I have stopped using a pH meter. I once tried to publish a paper about skipping pH adjustments with a popular gardening magazine but the topic was too controversial for them. pH was/is a topic they regularly turned to fill up their column inches with content–often articles written by their major advertisers.

I believe that time will tell that cannabis is like sunflowers–it has a very large pH range. This does require feeding the plants a high quality nutrient with chelated iron. More about chelates in chapter 10.

Nutrient solution pH should be allowed to drift up or down for both soilless and hydroponic growing systems. Letting the pH drift within reason provides opportunities for all of the various minerals within the solution to be absorbed and lets the plant choose what it takes in based on its needs, instead of force-feeding it with a strict, pH-driven regimen.

Testing pH

There are three common ways to check the pH of your nutrient solution: using a pH meter, litmus paper, or chemical indicator drops.

pH Meter

A pH meter is the easiest way to check pH. These electronic devices have a glass electrode that's paired to a digital display. Some also measure the temperature of the solution, and all have the one thing in common: you absolutely must read and follow the owner's manual. Be sure to keep pH meters cleaned and calibrated. An un-calibrated meter is useless, and a meter with nutrient solution built up on the probe will produce false readings.

- Pros: Easy to use
- Cons: Expensive, needs regular cleaning and calibration

Litmus Paper

Litmus paper is a simple way to measure pH. These paper strips, coated with pH-sensitive chemicals, change color when exposed to a solution. Simply tear off a piece and dunk it in the nutrient solution. Wait for it to change color and then compare to the included chart to "read" the pH.

- Pros: Inexpensive
- Cons: Must use litmus paper that measures the correct range (4.0-8.0), can be difficult to see subtle color differences, can degrade–needs to be used by expiration date

pH Testing Drops

Chemical pH-testing drops are similar to litmus paper as they also rely on a color change to indicate the pH of the tested solution. To use the chemical indicator drops, fill the small sample tube included with the test kit with the nutrient solution being tested, add as many testing drops as the manufacturer recommends, and shake. The solution will change color; compare the color to the included color chart to determine pH.

Dispose of the solution in the test vial by rinsing it thoroughly down the drain. NEVER pour it back into your nutrient reservoir, and NEVER add the drops directly into the reservoir–period.

- Pros: Cheap
- Cons: Can be difficult to see subtle color differences, can degrade–needs to be used by expiration date

Safely Adjusting pH Levels

Mishandling pH up and down solutions can be dangerous–these concentrated acids and bases cause chemical burns. When working with these solutions, be careful about these things:

- Wear safety glasses when adjusting pH. Splashing pH up or down solution into your eyes is dangerous. Best case, it's painful. Worst case, you have permanent eye damage. Always use eye protection when adjusting pH.
- Know where the closest water source and shower are, in case of a really big spill. The quicker you wash off the acid or base, the better.

Whenever you get a "strange" or unexpectedly out-of-range pH measurement from a meter, clean and calibrate it and try again. It's also a good idea to keep litmus paper or chemical indicator drops on hand to confirm erratic readings.

Bases (pH up) feel slimy on the hands. If your hands feel slimy after handling pH up, wash them immediately with LOTS of water. Chemical burns hurt for a long time– just say no!

If you're refilling a small bottle with pH up or down and it gets warm– you've topped up with the wrong solution. When acids and bases combine, they give off heat. Safely pour the mixture out, wash your hands and the bottle and start again.

- Decant large bottles into smaller, manageable ones. It does not matter how good of a pourer you are, pouring drops from a gallon bottle is never easy, especially when you're trying to be accurate. Use small bottles, preferably with flip tops, so it's easy to add lots or just a few drops. Make sure to clearly label them.
- Different manufacturers make different-strength pH up and down solutions–don't assume they are all the same. Some manufacturers pride themselves on making weak up/down as a safety precaution. Others brag about their solution being the strongest on the market because it's a better value. If the strength of the solution is not printed on the label, ask the retailer how strong the solution is, or look it up on the Internet. Regardless, when changing brands, use the new solution sparingly until you're familiar with its strength.
- If you decide to dilute a pH up or down solution, make sure you put the water into the bottle first and then pour in the acid/base. This is basic lab technique: if for some reason the acid/base breaks out into a reaction (unlikely, but possible), there's a small amount of acid/base in lots of water instead of a little bit of water with lots of acid/base in it to fly at you.
- For natural gardening, consider using citric acid for pH down and potassium bicarbonate for pH up.
- Commercial growers should consider purchasing concentrated acids and bases and dilute them. It's much cheaper than purchasing a diluted acid or base from a nutrient manufacturer.

Beneficial Organisms

Beneficial organisms, also known as "beneficials" or "bennies," include any organism that helps the plant. While this is a whole range of beings including birds, humans, and insects, generally the term bennies refer to soil-based microorganisms that provide a whole range of benefits to the host plant.

Beneficial organisms help translocate water within the grow media, colonize the roots to provide protection from invaders, and make nutrients available to the plant by moving minerals within the plant and chemically releasing "locked-up" ones. Beneficial organisms used indoors generally fall into three categories: funguses, bacteria, and nematodes.

- **Funguses** are the heavy lifters of the indoor beneficials. It's their job to break down heavy ligneous materials: the hard stuff trees and bushes are made from, called "brown material" by composters. Funguses form a symbiotic relationship with the roots and grow tiny calciferous tubes that transport water and nutrients from the soil to the roots. The most widely used indoor fungus are mycorrhizae and trichoderma.
- **Bacteria** are responsible for breaking down cellulose-based materials, what composters refer to as "green waste". They are much less mobile than fungus as they depend on the presence of water film to migrate. A commonly used indoor bacteria is bacillus subtilis.
- **Nematodes** are commonly deployed as a cure to a problem in the garden. They are very small worm-looking creatures that are known to attack over 200 different soil-based pests. For indoor gardens, nematodes can be used to control some of the nastiest pests such as fungus nats, thrips, and leaf miners.

The specific product used to introduce beneficial organisms to an indoor garden depends of the type of growing media used. In loose mixes, dry powder containing beneficials can be mixed in when planting clones or added when transplanting. Be careful to not smother young roots–adding too much power directly to the roots of a small clone can kill it.

In solid media, such as rockwool, beneficials can be watered in. There are specific products made for this purpose, if you're not sure about one, check with your local gardening shop or contact the product's manufacturer to make sure it should be used in this fashion.

Beneficial organisms are a very big part of the "soil food web," described by the famous and insightful garden writers Jeff Lowenfels and Wayne Lewis. They wrote an outstanding book called *Teaming with Microbes* that describes in plain language how beneficial organisms improve garden results; consider it a must-read.

Here are a few pointers to keep in mind with using beneficial organisms in your garden:

- Chlorine and chloramines in the water used for your nutrient solution will kill beneficial organisms. If you're using bennies, you must filter these compounds out of the water you use to feed your garden.
- Blackstrap molasses is a source of carbohydrates, potassium, calcium, and sometimes iron (check the label). Adding a teaspoon to a tablespoon per gallon to your nutrient solution is a great way to feed your beneficials and add flavor to your plants. Blackstrap molasses is not recommended for use in recycling hydroponic systems as it tends to foam up.
- Read and follow manufacturer's instructions to the letter when using products that include bennies—some have specific requirements including keeping them refrigerated.

Flushing

Flushing is a process by which excess nutrients are removed from the root zone. This is only a concern when using mineral salt-based nutrients and is generally not a useful technique when using organic nutrients. Organic nutrients tend to bond to the soil particles in very complex ways that flushing rarely affects. There are two reasons to flush your plants: correcting for overfeeding and clearing out nutrients from the grow media at the completion of the grow.

 Zen Gardening

If you properly feed your plants through the grow, there should be no reason to have to flush your plants either during the grow or at the end.

To correct for overfeeding, wash lots of water through the growing media. Generally, you'll need to use a volume of water that's two to four times the size of the plants' growing containers to flush. For instance, if you're growing in a 3-gallon pot, flush with 6-12 gallons of plain water–no nutrients.

Flushing at the end of the grow is simpler. In recirculating systems, just use plain water for the last week's "feeding". Some gardeners like to change the reservoir partway through the last week to ensure a thorough flush. In hand watering and run to waste systems, just feed the garden plain water during the final week.

Some gardeners use flushing solutions to aid in the process. These solutions contain sugars that help to break the bonds between the minerals and the growing media. Once these bonds are broken, the minerals are freed and can be washed out of the grow media.

Flushing has its limitations though. You can only remove salts in the grow media. Once a plant is overfed there is no way to flush it out. The only thing to do is flush the media, feed it very week nutrient and lower the light levels while they recover.

Salt Neutral

OK, so we have all heard about carbon neutral, but have you considered being "salt neutral"? Are the nutrients you're using mineral-salt based? How do you dispose of them? Most people dump salt-based nutrients down the drain and don't think much about it. This is a problem, since they are not completely removed at wastewater treatment plants. Over time these salts concentrate in our lands and water supplies. Mineral salt buildup is becoming such a serious threat in commercial agriculture that in certain regions, serious remediation techniques are being applied.

Hobby growers should consider going salt neutral with organic nutrients. Organics have come a long way from their introduction into the indoor garden market a few years ago. Early smell problems have been greatly reduced, and most newer formulations don't require pH adjustment. It's a win-win for the environment and you. Move over carbon: it's time for salt neutrality to take the spotlight!

Commercial growers should consider purchasing a wastewater reclamation system. Drain to waste adds a lot of nutrients into our sewer systems. I have been hearing horror stories about the amount of algae growth in sewers, lakes, and ponds. Many golf courses are now required to remove excess nitrogen from their runoff due to algae blooms in nearby lakes and streams. Soon these systems will be mandatory as the problem continues to get worse.

High-Quality Water

We've all heard the expression "garbage in, garbage out". The quality of the water you feed to your garden matters—a lot. The concentration of "the stuff" in water is measured in parts per million or ppm for short. The higher the ppm, the greater the amount of impurities in the water.

This "stuff" can bind with the nutrients in your reservoir, causing them to become locked up and unavailable to your plants. Water high in ppm's also contributes to the strength of your nutrient solution and can make an otherwise properly mixed feed solution too strong—thus overfeeding the plants.

 **EXPERT CORNER**

From an indoor gardening perspective, water quality is measured in "parts per million" or "ppm" for short. This is a reading of how many ions (such as calcium, magnesium, sodium, lead, etc.) are present in the water.

A 10 ppm reading means that there are 10 ions per one million water molecules.

You need to start with good-quality water, either purchased or filtered, of not more than ~100 ppm. As mentioned before, no matter what else you do, you must remove the chlorine and chloramines from your feed solution when growing with beneficials. Chlorine is very harmful to beneficial organisms and will reduce or eliminate their colonies.

Before you decide on your filtration needs, test your water with a "ppm meter" available from your local indoor gardening center. It's also a good idea to contact your local water management office for a water report. This will give you a good idea of the quality of your water and whether there are changes in the water supply during the year. For example, some municipalities use local ground water for most of the year, but during certain times imported water is mixed into local supplies, changing the mix of water-borne elements significantly. Changes in the composition of your water supply could explain incurable pH swings or nutrient precipitation (sludge) in your reservoir.

Filtration

It's always a good idea to filter the water you use for gardening, regardless of its quality. The initial hardness (ppm) of the water will dictate the filtration strategy–reverse osmosis or carbon filtration. Reverse-osmosis filters are used when your water quality is fair to poor–more than ~100 ppm of dissolved minerals. Use a carbon filter when the source water has an initial ppm reading of under 100.

Reverse osmosis (R/O) water is produced by a filter system that uses pressure to force water through a membrane that traps and rejects contaminants, which are discarded as a wastewater stream. R/O units are rated by how much wastewater to clean water they produce. Cheap units waste a lot of water, with waste-to-good ratios as high as 5:1. Efficient units can run as low as 1:5 or less. Many of the newer systems can produce water that is very clean–down to a few ppm–though as the ratio of good water to wastewater drops closer to 1:5, R/O filters may require quite a bit of electricity. Contact the manufacturer to get exact performance specifications; good suppliers are happy to supply this info.

Carbon filters are a less expensive alternative to R/O systems if your water source does not have very many impurities. Carbon filters remove chlorine and chloramines, but that's about it. The best thing about these filters is that they produce no wastewater.

If you're using well water, you need to take extra care because well water can contain unknown amounts of impurities (calcium, magnesium, sodium, carbonates, sulfates, etc.), plus pathogens such as bacteria, viruses, and other microorganisms that can cause disease. While an R/O filter can remove unwanted mineral impurities, it won't filter out pathogens.

To clean up well water, use a water filter that exposes the water to ultraviolet light, particularly UV-C. UV-C is very good at killing viruses and bacteria. Run your R/O-cleaned water through a separate UV-C filter if you're using well water or buy a combination R/O and UV-C filter setup. Most people who live on well water already have methods to filter and sterilize their water.

Alkaline vs. Alkalinity

Many people get confused about the difference between alkaline and alkalinity or think they're the same thing. They're not. Alkaline means having a pH greater than 7 (also called "basic"), while alkalinity is the concentration of ions in a substance (such as sulfates, phosphates, silicates, or carbonates), measured in ppm. The classic example comparing alkaline and alkalinity is that the pH (alkaline level) of a solution can be lowered by dissolving CO_2 into it, while the alkalinity (ppm) of the solution remains unchanged.

If you're using R/O water, consider blending in a little dechlorinated city water. The city water's alkalinity helps to buffer pH fluctuations in your nutrient solution. Most hydroponic nutrient manufacturers assume you are using water with some alkalinity. Consider 60-80 initial ppm to be a good starting point for your water blend and experiment from there.

Other Lab Techniques

Every serious indoor gardener should consider taking a college-level general chemistry course, *and the lab*–even if you consider yourself a "liberal arts" type. Heck I'm a science major and published three books so stop making excuses!

There is so much interesting science to learn, but more importantly, you'll learn lab techniques that improve safety, save money and time, and make your garden more successful. Some of the products we use in our gardens are expensive, and we don't want to waste them due to simple mixing and handling errors.

Tips you'll learn in chemistry lab include:

- Never pour back into a bottle. Period. Any bottle. Trying to save a bit by pouring any excess back into the bottle is <u>NEVER</u> a good idea. The little amount you're saving presents a big risk of contaminating the whole bottle.
- Wash your hands before and after mixing any nutrients, just like your mother had you do before eating. This simple technique helps prevent contamination.
- Mix in the reservoir, not in the measuring cup. There is a reason hydroponic nutrient manufacturers split some formulas into multiple parts. It's because many of the compounds that are stored in separate bottles will react with compounds in the other bottles if they are exposed to each other at full strength. When they react, the minerals bind together and become unavailable to the plants, causing incomplete nutrition. When multi-part nutrient solutions are mixed into a reservoir that provides sufficient dilution, the reactions between the minerals in the various bottles are slowed or stopped altogether.
- Put tops on bottles right away. This might sound trivial, but we all have knocked over bottles.
- Don't rinse the nutrient/pH solution cap in the nutrient reservoir. Some growers like to use the bottle top as a measuring cup. For some reason, after they measure out what they need, many of these gardeners decided to rinse the cap by swishing it in the nutrient reservoir. This is a *really* bad idea as it contaminates the rest of the bottle and possibly the reservoir, too.

10. What to Feed Plants

There are many well-written books about plant nutrition; you should read several. This chapter isn't meant to replace any of them. Instead, it examines plant nutrition from the perspective of an amateur gardener who's looking at a nutrient bottle or box and trying to make sense of it. For each of the primary, secondary, and micronutrients, we'll discuss what the nutrient does inside a plant and how that translates into the specific types of nutrient compounds that best address these needs. Let's start at the very beginning:

EXPERT CORNER

Don't believe the heavily promoted myth that flowering plants need less nitrogen during the flowering phase. Many of them need more nitrogen in flower, not less.

How to Read a Nutrient Label

Deciphering the label on a nutrient bottle or box can be a daunting task. There are so many different formulas, many claiming explosive growth, or increased yields over their competitors. Trying to compare them side by side may not reveal much unless you know what to look for.

By state law, which of course varies state to state, nutrient manufacturers are required to include *some* specific information about what's contained into the product. Many other compounds are also contained in most products, but since they are not specifically required to be listed, they're not.

Nutrient labeling regulations are so complicated that it's not unusual for products from reputable companies to get pulled from the market because their labels don't conform to labeling requirements in some way.

The table at the end of this chapter will come in handy while you're trying to make sense of a nutrient label. Use it as a reference when reading the rest of this chapter. It lists the elements needed by plants with their chemical forms plus common compounds that contain them.

Primary Nutrients (N, P, K)

Nitrogen, phosphorus, and potassium, commonly referred to as "N-P-K" or the "big three," are the primary nutrients for plants. They are considered the "meat and potatoes" of plant nutrition—elements that are heavily used by plants at every stage of their life cycle.

Nitrogen (N)

Nitrogen is available to plants in two forms; ammoniacal nitrogen (NH_4^+) and nitrate nitrogen (NO_3^-) with nitrate nitrogen being the preferred form for indoor gardening. Nitrogen is the most abundant element we feed to our plants. Carbon, hydrogen, and oxygen are found in higher quantities in plant tissue, but they are derived by the plant from carbon dioxide and water, not fed to the plant by gardeners. Nitrogen is the basis for many of the plant's complex compounds such as chlorophyll, amino acids, proteins, ATP, and even DNA. Without nitrogen, plant life could not happen.

In nature there are two ways a plant can obtain nitrogen. The first is by fixing atmospheric nitrogen (N_2) though the use of an Azotobacter. Azotobacters are bacteria that convert the nitrogen in the air into ammonium ions (NH_4^+) that can be directly fed to the plant or passed to the soil for further processing. The second way is through a process called ammonification. This is where dead plants and animals are broken down (decay) into ammonium, which is also either taken up by the plant or passed into the soil for further processing.

So what's this further processing? It's a process called nitrification that converts ammonium ions (NH_4^+) into nitrate (NO_3^-) through two different forms of bacteria: Nitrosomonas and Nitrobacters.

$$NH_4^+ + Nitrosomonas \rightarrow NO_2^- + Nitrobacter \rightarrow NO_3^-$$

One of the ways indoor gardens are different than those found in nature is that we feed indoor gardens from bottles and don't rely on decaying plants and microorganisms to feed the garden. All the nutritional elements we feed to the plants have to be "readily available", meaning that they are in a form that is easy for the plant to take in and use.

Thus, there are several different forms of nitrogen, with varying levels of availability. Complicating matters, nitrogen is also labeled in many different ways. Here are two examples of how nitrogen shows up on nutrient bottle labels:

```
Total nitrogen...................................................................5%
    Ammoniacal nitrogen..........................................1%
    Water insoluble nitrogen.....................................2%
    Water soluble nitrogen........................................2%
```

```
Total nitrogen...................................................................2%
    Nitrate nitrogen.................................................1.5%
    Urea nitrogen.....................................................0.3%
    Ammoniacal nitrogen.........................................0.2%
```

- Ammoniacal nitrogen can be directly used by plants. It's critical that you understand that plants can't regulate the uptake of the ammoniacal form of nitrogen; if it's present, they will absorb it. If the plant is not capable of creating and transporting enough carbohydrates to the roots to process this nitrogen, ammoniacal nitrogen can overwhelm the plant, causing harm. Be careful when using fertilizers high in ammoniacal nitrogen, especially in hydroponic media. The effect is somewhat reduced in soil/soilless media, as the positively charged ammonia ion has the potential to bond with the negatively charged soil particles.

- Water insoluble nitrogen is a slow-release form of nitrogen. It must be broken down by microorganisms in the grow media before it can be used by the plants.
- Water soluble nitrogen is just as it sounds–it's all the soluble and readily available forms of nitrogen lumped together. These can include (and not be specifically labeled as) ammoniacal, nitrate, soluble and readily available forms of nitrogen and urea.

Fun Fact

NH_4^+ (ammonium) form of nitrogen lowers soil pH and NO_3^- (nitrate) form of nitrogen raises soil pH.

- Nitrate nitrogen can be directly used by plants and is the preferred form for indoor use.
- Stay away from urea in indoor gardening. Urea needs to be converted to a usable form by an enzyme called urease, which is not typically found in indoor grow media.

Phosphorus (P)

Phosphorus is essential for plant life as it's a component of DNA, chlorophyll, phospholipids, nucleotides, and coenzymes–a lot of the stuff that makes plants work. It's involved in stimulating root development, increasing stem and stalk strength, improving flower formation, and increasing resistance to plant diseases.

Like nitrogen, phosphorus has different forms. Generally in indoor gardening we use phosphorous in the phosphate (Pi) form, which is derived from phosphoric acid (H_3PO_4).

Another form called phosphite (Phi) is derived from phosphorous acid (H_3PO_3). For indoor gardening, phosphite has very limited use. It's used by big agriculture as a fungicide and not as a source of phosphorus. Stay away from products that contain phosphite when growing indoors. You can identify them by looking for "derived from phosphorous acid" on the label.

If the effects of phosphorus on plants were discovered in more modern times, or at least after analytical chemistry techniques were available, it most likely would not be considered one of the macro elements. It remains considered one of the "big three" more due to when its effects were discovered than the amount used by plants. Tissue analysis and soil sampling has determined that plants use significantly more nitrogen and potassium than phosphorus. This ratio holds true for most plants with both vegetative and flowering states.

Too much phosphorus can kill beneficial microorganisms such as mycorrhizae. Additionally, excessive phosphorus can cause copper, iron, manganese, and zinc deficiencies. Typically, plants require phosphorus at a rate similar to their requirements of calcium or magnesium.

A big trend in indoor gardening is to use "bloom boosters" during a plant's flowering cycle that are heavy in phosphorus and potassium. Bloom boosters come in an array of products that contain little to no nitrogen, extremely large amounts of phosphorus, and quite a bit of potassium. To identify them, look for N-P-K labeling such as "0-50-30". High levels of potassium are great for flowering plants, but plants don't require nearly the amount of phosphorus contained in the typical bloom booster and can be burned by the excess. High phosphorus bloom boosters should be used only by experienced gardeners.

Phosphorus is labeled as P_2O_5 by law, but that's a bit misleading. See the Commercial versus Elemental Analysis at the end of the chapter for details.

Potassium (K)

Potassium's role in plants is a bit different than the role of other nutrients. It's not actually part of any plant structures, but it assists with most of the functions within a plant. Potassium, also referred to as potash, is often called the "quality nutrient" because of its positive effects of fruiting size, shape, color, taste, and other quality measurements. Some of the other effects of potassium are:

- Increases enzyme production and activation
- Helps relocation of plant sugars and starches
- Regulates of stomata for water retention
- Accelerates root growth
- Aids with photosynthesis and protein synthesis
- Improves drought tolerance
- Helps defend against crop diseases
- Assists in ion balance control

 **Sloper Says**

Plant nutrition does not change dramatically when converting from vegetative to flowering states. I have personally used the same formula of nutrients for both the veg and flower.

I know plenty of commercial growers that use the same single powder-based nutrient in both grow and bloom stages without a single additive and produce excellent results. Their methods have been shown effective in everything from soil to rockwool.

Basically what I am saying is that a big bunch of the bottles in the hydroponics shops are a waste of money. Generally, learning better gardening techniques through experience is going to give you better results than buying expensive bottles.

Potassium is labeled as K_2O as required by law, but that's a bit misleading. See the Commercial Analysis versus Elemental Analysis section for more information on potassium concentrations.

Secondary Nutrients (Ca, Mg, S)

Calcium, magnesium, and sulfur are classified as secondary nutrients. They are called this because they are consumed in smaller amounts than the primary nutrients but in greater amounts than the seven micronutrients. Secondary nutrients play critical roles and are just as important as NPK.

Calcium (Ca)

Plants, just like humans, need calcium. In humans, calcium builds strong teeth and bones. Similarly, in plants, calcium forms calcium pectate which strengthens cell walls and allows them to bind together. It's a critical element in overall plant growth and has been identified as a factor in increasing nitrogen uptake. Calcium is translocated through the plant via transportation. Other benefits of calcium are:

- Major component in photosynthesis, critical in the light-dependent reactions that split water molecules
- Disease prevention–strong cell walls can ward off attack by fungus and bacteria
- Stimulation of the protein channels that take up nutrients
- Aids in plant signaling and intracellular regulation
- Stomata regulation and heat stress relief
- Improves fruit quality

Magnesium (Mg)

Magnesium is critical for plants. It is found in every cell type in all living things–plants, animals, bacteria, and fungus. In plants it serves as the central molecule in chlorophyll and enables productive carbohydrate synthesis. It's also a catalyst for certain enzyme activity–specifically in converting sucrose into glucose and fructose. Some other functions of magnesium are:

- Binds with RuBisCO for activation
- Transportation of phosphorus in the plant
- Starch/sugar translocation
- Plant oil and fat formation
- Nutrient uptake control
- Increased iron utilization

Sulfur (S)

Interestingly enough, sulfur often gets overlooked as a plant nutrient. The big three, NPK, are at the forefront. Next to be recognized are calcium and magnesium–probably because they're sold together in a bottle. Even silicon is better known to indoor gardeners. Sulfur is almost always thought of as a fungicide but rarely discussed as a nutrient–strange for an element that is used by plants almost as much as phosphorus. Some of the major functions of sulfur are:

- Synthesis of vitamins
- Synthesis of some amino acids
- Production of proteins
- Chlorophyll formation

Micronutrients

Micronutrients are just what they sound like: nutrients that are used in small amounts in compared to the rest. They're also called trace elements or "micros". Although they are used in small quantities, they are critical. Without them, your garden won't produce well and will eventually die. Unless you're using very bad grow media or cheap nutrients, deficiencies of micronutrients only occur at extreme (either too high or too low) pH levels.

Boron (B)

Our current knowledge about boron's role in plants is very limited, though recent studies have helped to unlock its purpose in plant growth. Boron has been linked to several critical plant processes, including cell differentiation, cell wall formation, and carbohydrate synthesis. Boron has also been shown to be essential for flowering and pollen production.

Plants use very little boron, and too much is toxic. The effective amount of boron is very small, so be careful when using fertilizers with more than trace amounts of it. Like Calcium, Boron is translocated through the plant via transportation. Generally, most indoor gardeners don't need to worry about boron toxicities or deficiencies if they are using high-quality plant fertilizers.

EXPERT CORNER

Many of the micronutrients found in plant nutrient bottles come in a "chelated" form. Chelated forms enable the element to be available to the plant in a broader pH range and to be more stable within the plant.

Elements in chelated forms can be identified by names that contain suffixes such as EDTA, EDDHA, and DTPA.

Chlorine (Cl)

Chlorine is a bit of a misnomer. While chlorine is the name of the element (and how it's labeled), it's not what plants actually consume. Plants make use of chloride (Cl^-), a different, reduced form of chlorine. Nonetheless, it's listed as chlorine on nutrient labels due to labeling regulations.

Chlorine works in tandem with potassium to control stomata opening and closing, critical for the plant to regulate water and CO_2 levels. It also aids in photosynthesis, specifically in the light-dependent reactions, and is responsible for some of the nutrient transport functions within the plant.

Cobalt (Co)

Very little is known about cobalt's role in higher plants. The only known physiological role of cobalt in plants is its involvement in nitrogen fixing by leguminous plants such as green beans. Cobalt is often regarded as a "non-essential"–more on non-essentials at the end of this chapter. It is interesting that many major nutrient manufacturers include cobalt in their formulations even though its role is not understood.

Copper (Cu)

Copper's largest role in plant nutrition is as a catalyst in photosynthesis and transpiration, and it's a constituent of several enzymes that build amino acids and convert them to proteins. Copper is also important to the formation of lignin in plant cell walls and is known to affect flavor and carbohydrate content.

Iron (Fe)

Iron is essential for the formation of chlorophyll, is a component of cytochromes, is required for nitrogen-fixation processes, and helps to regulate plant transpiration. Like many of the other essential elements used by plants, it has more than one form. Fe^{2+}, also called "ferrous" iron, is the form that's most available to plants at normal pH ranges.

As the pH of the grow media rises, Fe^{2+} can become unavailable to plants. In the real world, iron deficiency is usually not a problem, unless you've managed to get the pH of your root zone completely off base.

EXPERT CORNER

Fe^{2+} converts to Fe^{3+} at higher pH ranges. Fe^{3+} is not a readily available form for plants. For this reason, extremely high pH can cause a deficiency in iron.

Manganese (Mn)

Manganese facilitates the assimilation of CO_2 during photosynthesis, the synthesis of chlorophyll, and the absorption of nitrogen. It also plays a role in the creation of riboflavin and carotenes. Like iron, manganese is unavailable to plants at higher pH levels. Thus, manganese and iron deficiencies often occur together.

Molybdenum (Mo)

Molybdenum (pronounced "mō-LEB-da-num") has a small but important role in plant growth. Its main function is the conversion of nitrates (NO_3^-) into amino acids, which are the building blocks of proteins. Molybdenum is also essential to the conversion of non-available phosphorus into available forms.

A note of caution–make sure to not feed plants that were grown using fertilizers containing molybdenum to livestock. Molybdenum causes infertility of livestock in low concentrations and severe diarrhea and rough coats at high concentrations. Good news for our hooved friends, these conditions can be treated with copper supplementation.

Zinc (Zn)

Zinc is highly versatile: it's an essential component of various enzymes, is used in protein synthesis and growth regulation, aids the production of auxin, regulates starch formation, and helps with root development. Additionally, zinc enables plants to withstand lower temperatures.

"Non-Essentials"

In addition to the elements that are directly involved in plant nutrition and function, other nutrients are often found in plant tissues. They are classified as non-essential but still may have noticeable benefits when applied. These include aluminum, sodium, selenium, silicon, rubidium, strontium, fluorine, vanadium, and iodine, plus certain vitamins.

Silicon

Silicon is the only non-essential element worth mentioning in detail. Even though it's not directly used by the plant, it is found in very high concentrations within plant tissue–rivaling the levels of nitrogen and potassium. Silicon strengthens cell walls, making the plant less susceptible to insect and fungal attacks. Silicon also improves soil structures, allowing better uptake of micronutrients.

Most hydroponic nutrients do not generally include silicon in their basic formulas, so you'll have to add it separately to your garden's feeding regimen. For those running "solid" grow media such as

 **Fun Fact**

Silicon is found in high concentrations in trichomes, which are small hairs and other structures that grow on the outer surface of a plant. Silicon is responsible for the strength and surface texture of the trichomes.

rockwool or expanded clay, liquid silicon can be added from a bottle. Look for the term "potassium silicate" on the label, and you'll know you're using the right stuff.

For those growing in "loose" grow media such as a soilless mix, consider mixing a natural source of silicon into the mix such as diatomaceous earth (DE). DE is comprised of ancient fossilized diatoms, which are a class of algae. It's sold under various names, including Diatomite and Hygromite. There are two basic forms of DE: pebble-sized solid rocks, and powder. Both can be blended into almost any loose grow media. The solid form can be a cost saver since it can be reused after a good cleaning.

The powdered version of DE is also used as for pest control. It kills a bunch of garden pests, including white flies, ants, mites, fleas, and leafhoppers. A thin layer of powdered diatomaceous earth applied to the top of the grow media will help stop pest outbreaks, since its glass-shard structure shreds the exoskeleton of any pest that comes in contact with it–killing them fast. It's completely safe for humans and pets: "food grade" DE is sold in health food stores for human consumption as an aid to health, and in pet stores to control fleas both on animals and in their bedding.

Make sure any diatomaceous earth you use comes from freshwater sources, NOT saltwater sources. With high sodium levels, saltwater DE can quickly turn your grow media toxic. The big hardware stores often sell "pool-grade" DE, which is generally the saltwater version of DE. Pool-grade DE has also been subjected to very high temperatures, converting it to the crystalline form that makes a very good water filter but is dangerous to inhale. Make sure any DE you buy for use in the garden is labeled for use as an insecticide or as food grade.

 **Sloper Says**

If growing in expanded clay, consider using a 50:50 ratio of expanded clay and diatomaceous earth rocks–you will love the results.

In addition to DE, there are other powdered forms of silicon that can be incorporated into your grow media. These fall into a category called "rock dust". Rock dust is a common by-product of the gravel industry: it's generated when rocks get crushed. While most rock dust comes from limestone, there are other sources, including volcanic and glacial deposits. In addition to silicon, rock dust powders often provide secondary and trace elements. The actual nutrients in a specific batch of rock dust depend on where it was mined. Glacial rock dust, greensand, and Azomite are common names for these types of products.

It's simple to conduct your own experiments to see whether rock dust or diatomaceous earth is effective for your garden or to see which one is best for your garden's needs. Simply add some to one or two plants when growing several of the same species and leave the rest as the control group. Do everything exactly the same as before but keep an eye on your experimental plants–you might be pleasantly surprised at the results.

Vitamin B

Several vitamins are also beneficial to plants. Vitamin B is probably the most discussed vitamin used in indoor gardening. Many nutrient manufacturers include B1–also known as thiamine–somewhere in their lineup of bottles. Based on laboratory tests conducted in the 1930's, Vitamin B purportedly reduces transplant shock, promotes root development, and aids in plant growth.

Many university researchers, including Robert Cox, horticulture agent at Colorado State University Cooperative Extension and author of the report "Beware of Gardening Myths," have studied B1. Outside of the lab, in tests designed to measure the impact of B1 on whole plants instead of tissue samples, B1 shows no discernible effect on plant growth. Nutrient products containing B1 typically also include minerals and sometimes plant hormones that may cause treated plants to perform better than untreated plants. But the effects in this case are due to the other ingredients, not the B1.

Vitamin C

Plants, like animals, use Vitamin C for a range of metabolic processes. In plants, Vitamin C is found in the chloroplasts–the cells in which photosynthesis occurs. It acts as an antioxidant, protecting the plant from pollutants and free radicals released by various metabolic processes.

Even though most plants and animals (except humans) produce sufficient supplies of Vitamin C internally to support growth, studies have shown that supplemental Vitamin C increases growth. In 1935, Synnöve and Hausen published a study showing that 40 mg of Vitamin C added to a sterile liquid growing medium increased the dry weight of the treated plants over control plants by 35 to 75%.

Vitamin D

Just as humans, plants can synthesize their own Vitamin D. Vitamin D has been associated with adventitious root growth (roots forming in new places) as well as calcium transport. In a 1979 paper, Buchala and Schmid suggested that Vitamin D should be part of a new class of plant growth stimulators because of its effectiveness. Currently, there are no nutrients that list Vitamin D as an ingredient, though due to labeling requirements, it might be in the bottle but not disclosed as an ingredient.

Oxidization State and Nutrient Availability

In addition to pH, nutrient availability is also linked to the oxidization state of the element. An oxidization state is a number assigned to an element when combined in a compound that describes how a compound is expected to react with other compounds in a chemical reaction. Since plants absorb nutrients via chemical reactions, the oxidization state of the nutrients directly affects their ability to be absorbed.

The table on the next page lists three critical elements for plant growth–nitrogen, phosphorus and iron–along with forms (compounds) in which these elements are commonly used in plant nutritional formulas. It shows why certain compounds simply don't work for plant nutrition… it turns out plants just don't use elements in a +3 oxidization state!

Element	Form	Oxidization State	Used by Plants
Nitrogen	Ammonium (NH_4^+)	-3	Yes
	Nitrite (NO_2^-)	+3	No
	Nitrate (NO_3^-)	+5	Yes
Phosphorus	Phosphate (PO_4^{3-})	+5	Yes
	Phosphite (PO_3^{3-})	+3	No
Iron	Iron II (Fe^{2+})	+2	Yes
	Iron III (Fe^{3+})	+3	No

Limiting Reagent

Growing under high light conditions (1200+ PPFD) requires all the grow room parameters to be correct. These include light quality and quantity, temperature, humidity, CO_2 and nutrients. If any one of them is off, the overall process of plant growth is slowed. It's critical to keep up on all of them: the garden's ability to thrive will be reduced to/limited by the parameter that is the most "off". This parameter becomes the garden's "lowest common denominator" (in math speak) or "limiting reagent" (in chemistry speak).

Following the limiting reagent example, let's assume a chemical reaction that requires 2 molecules of X and 1 molecule Y to make the final product. If you have 5 of each you can only make 2 total products – X will be the limiting reagent.

The main problem I encounter is that nutritional strength is not increased when light levels are increased. Nutrition then becomes the limiting reagent: without enough nutrition, the plants won't be able to convert all that light into carbohydrates needed to produce heavy harvests. They will suffer and the increased photon density provided to them wasted.

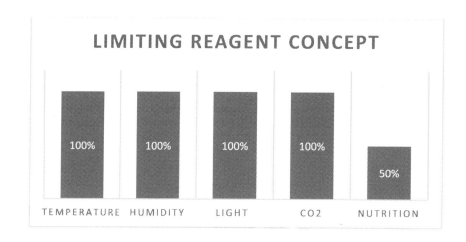

Note: garden performance is limited by inadequate nutrition

Commercial vs. Elemental Analysis

Every bottle or bag of plant fertilizer has three large numbers prominently displayed on the label, such as 10-10-10. These numbers indicate the percentage of the "big three" nutrients included in the fertilizer: 10% nitrogen, 10% phosphorous and 10% potassium. But this is one case where "what you see is not what you get", due to another issue with how fertilizers are labeled.

It turns out that labeling rules require phosphorous and potassium to be listed in their oxidized forms, meaning that the compound that's being tested includes other molecules besides the elemental phosphorous and potassium plants use. The actual levels of usable phosphorus and potassium in any fertilizer are quite a bit lower than the percentage listed on the label.

Let's look at that 10-10-10 fertilizer again. Nitrogen gets its full weight since labeling requirements allow it to be measured in its elemental form. Elemental phosphorus is only 4.36% of total weight and elemental potassium is 8.30%, once the extra molecules plants don't eat are removed from the equation. Thus that bottle labeled 10-10-10 is really 10.0-4.4-8.3, based on the <u>elemental</u> weight of NPK.

Why is this important? Because you'll be better equipped to deal with nutritional deficiencies and toxicities when you need to understand how the fertilizers you're using are formulated. You could be accidentally under- or over-feeding your garden if you rely on the percentages listed on plant fertilizer packaging without understanding what they mean. Also, the fact that bio-available phosphorous and potassium in any plant food is quite a bit lower than what's listed on the label helps to explain why few gardeners poison their gardens with bloom boosters, since the products aren't as heavy in phosphorus as they could be! (0-50-30 bloom booster elementally is really only 0-21.8-24.9)

For the geeks, here is a bit of chemistry: to convert the oxides to the elemental concentrations we must first consult a periodic table to obtain the atomic weights. We find that oxygen's atomic weight is 16, phosphorus is 31, and potassium is 39. With that it's just some simple math to get to the truth. Basically divide the weight of the element in question by the total weight of the oxide.

How much elemental phosphorus is contained in P_2O_5?

$$\left(\frac{P_2}{P_2O_5}\right) = \left(\frac{P+P}{P+P+O+O+O+O+O}\right) = \left(\frac{31+31}{31+31+16+16+16+16+16}\right) =$$

0.436 or 43.6% elemental phosphorus

How much elemental potassium is contained in K_2O?

$$\left(\frac{K_2}{K_2O}\right) = \left(\frac{K+K}{K+K+O}\right) = \left(\frac{39+39}{39+39+16}\right) =$$

0.830 or 83.0% elemental potassium

Reference chart for deciphering a nutrient bottle:

	Element	Chemical Form	Common Compounds
Primary	Nitrogen (N)	NO_3^-, NH_4^+	Ammonium nitrate, potassium nitrate
	Phosphorous (P)	$H_2PO_4^-$, HPO_4^{2-}	Potassium phosphate, ammonium phosphate
	Potassium (K)	K^+	Potassium nitrate, potassium chloride
Secondary	Calcium (Ca)	Ca^{2+}	Calcium nitrate, calcium chloride
	Magnesium (Mg)	Mg^{2+}	Magnesium nitrate, magnesium sulfate
	Sulfur (S)	SO_4^{2-}	Zinc sulfate, cobalt sulfate
Micronutrients	Boron (B)	$H_2BO_3^-$	Potassium borate, borax, boric acid
	Chlorine (Cl)	Cl^-	Calcium chloride, potassium chloride
	Cobalt (Co)*	Co^{2+}	Cobalt sulfate, cobalt EDTA
	Copper (Cu)*	Cu^{2+}	Copper sulfate, copper EDTA
	Iron (Fe)*	Fe^{2+}	Iron sulfate, ferrous sulfate, iron EDTA, iron DTPA
	Manganese (Mn)*	Mn^{2+}	Manganese EDTA, manganese sulfate
	Molybdenum (Mo)	MoO_4^{2-}	Ammonium molybdate, sodium molybdate
	Zinc (Zn)*	Zn^{2+}	Zinc EDTA, zinc sulfate
	* May be chelated		

11. Pest Prevention

There are many great books written specifically about plant pests and diseases. This chapter is <u>not</u> a replacement for them: it's a primer to jumpstart your thinking about protecting your investment in your garden, as well as an opportunity for me to pass along some tips.

Pest prevention for indoor gardens can be a challenge even for the most experienced gardener, especially under burple LEDs because small, telltale signs of an infection can be masked and overlooked. Here are a few tactics to consider for your grow's pest management plan.

✿ Good Practice

A note to the commercial crowd– make sure to stay informed on what pest prevention techniques are allowable for the crop your growing. I hear far too many stories that an entire harvest got destroyed because someone sprayed something that was not suitable for that crop type or banned in that location.

Sticky Traps

Before you can eradicate pests from your garden, you must first identify them. Sticky traps are a great way to determine whether you're dealing with flying pests and if so, which ones. These traps come in various versions depending on the pests they target. The most common ones for indoor gardening are either yellow or blue: yellow is for whiteflies, aphids, and other flying insects, blue for thrips and leafminers. Most gardeners keep sticky traps near the plants' stems at every stage of plant development to provide continual surveillance for flying pests.

So what colored clothes should you avoid wearing when visiting/working at a grow? Blue and yellow. Just as blue and yellow attract bugs to sticky cards, blue and yellow clothing will attract bugs when walking outside. Thrips exist everywhere and would love to catch a ride into a grow.

Once you've trapped some pests and know what you're combating, you can develop a strategy to wipe them out. If you've trapped some bugs but don't know what they are, take the trap to a garden center or hydroponic shop so they can help with identification and treatment. Do everyone a favor and place it in a plastic bag, so you don't spread the infestation.

Air Filtration

Many of the problems in our gardens come in from the outside during air exchanges. Small pests, fungi, and bacteria can all make their way into the garden though air vents. When using a powered intake fan, consider using a HEPA filter to eliminate this potential source of pests–and change this filter at least once per quarter. HEPA filters are usually too restrictive to be used with passive vents. If you experience a pest problem in a small garden with passive intake vents, cover the vents with a nylon stocking or "batting" purchased at a fabric store to help keep the little buggers out.

Beneficial Predators

Maybe I am a total geek but I love watching that black-and-white Japanese movie where Mothra and Godzilla battle it out. Every time I release beneficial predators in a garden that movie comes to mind. In this case predators are good. Their job is to eat harmful invaders and not damage the garden. There are several bugs that indoor gardeners enlist depending on the type of infestation. The sooner predators are released the better chance they have to do their job.

Predator Mites

Predator mites do exactly what their name implies–they eat mites. There are many species of predator mites all with their unique habits and preferred environmental conditions (temperature and humidity). Predator mites typically consume five to ten mites or twenty eggs per day. But that's not their main advantage–they usually reproduce twice as fast as spider mites so can quickly overwhelm them. Predator mites are voracious little creatures that need to eat often or they will die off.

 **EXPERT CORNER**

Female spider mites can go dormant for weeks. This is why outbreaks can reemerge after you're sure they have been eradicated.

Spider mite and Russet mite populations are becoming increasingly problematic in indoor gardens. There are a few different strains of predatory mites that really go to town on the bad mites. *Mesoseiulus longpipes, Neoseiulus californicus, Phytoseiulus persimilis, and Amblyseius andersoni* all do a very good job cleaning up those problematic mites. Keep in mind when purchasing these guys they will either come live (so pick them up and release them right away) or in breeder sachets (that require more attention and instruction on hatching eggs). It is recommended that predatory mites be released once per week for three weeks and once more 30 days after the last release.

Praying Mantis

Of all the predators used in indoor gardening, praying mantis have to be the most entertaining. They are a fantastic predator as they eat most garden pests. Praying mantis are born from egg casings that contain up to two hundred young ones. When young they eat smaller pests such as aphids (and their eggs), caterpillars and mites. As they age, they can consume larger insects such as beetles, crickets and grasshoppers.

Praying Mantis lie and wait for their food. When close enough, they snap prey up with lightning fast movement of their strong forelegs. They react more than twice as fast as houseflies.

Green Lacewings

Green lacewings love to munch on common garden pests such as aphids, thrips, mealybugs and whiteflies in their larval stages. They kill by injecting a paralyzing venom then sucking the body fluids from their helpless insect victim. As they age their diet switches from insects to nectars and pollens.

There is much diversity among lacewings—around two thousand species. Some of them are capable of devouring two hundred aphids a week. These guys will hang around and if the conditions are right they will lay eggs on silk threads hanging from under the leaf. Green Lacewings are the best all-around predator for gardens.

Ladybugs

Ladybugs, also known as lady beetles and ladybird beetles, are a group of beneficial insects that consume a great number of indoor pests including mites, leafhoppers, scales, mealy bugs, aphids, and other soft-bodied insects. Ladybugs are best employed early in an outbreak.

Good news for LED-based growers: ladybugs are LED friendly. Anyone who has made the mistake of releasing ladybugs into a grow space with exposed HID lamps (not protected by a glass lens) knows that the ladybugs, attracted by the light and heat, will fly straight up into the HID lights and burn up—what a smell! Worse than burned hair. This is *not a problem* with LEDs. The color of the light is not as attractive to ladybugs, plus the lights don't get hot enough to fry them. Most commercial growers that I know do not use ladybugs as there are more effective alternatives.

Spraying

Many indoor pest infestations are solved by spraying with a substance that will kill the bugs but not ruin your crop. But what to use? Different pest treatments attack different predators, so it's important to know both that pest(s) you need to eradicate and the options for safely killing them. Some pesticides break down into compounds that are poisonous if consumed or burned: if your crop is destined for human consumption, be sure to select pest treatments that do not leave toxic residue.

Here are a few pest sprays that are generally considered safe for crops grown indoors.

Sulfur

Earlier we discussed plants' nutritional need for sulfur. Sulfur has another application in indoor gardening: it's a fungicide used to fight against mold and fungus outbreaks like black spot, powdery mildew and rust. It's also effective against mites and thrips. Sulfur is probably the oldest known pesticide used today.

Indoors, sulfur can be directly sprayed or vaporized into the air to settle onto the plants. If vaporizing, make sure no one is in the grow room as sulfur can be harmful to the lungs if inhaled. It's considered honeybee safe and acceptable in most organic applications. Don't use sulfur on pants that have been treated with spray oils within the last 30 days as it can react with them and cause more harm than good. Also don't apply sulfur when temperatures exceed 80°F/27°C. Sulfur should only be used on cannabis when flowers are not present.

Azadirachtin (Neem Oil Extract)

Azadirachtin is an oil that is extracted from neem seeds and is fantastic for controlling garden pests. It's available under many names with some brands add additional pest-fighting ingredients. Azadirachtin should be used as your first line of defense against pests and funguses that take up residence in your garden. It acts as an insecticide, miticide, nematicide and fungicide, thus correcting many common indoor gardening infestations. Pure azadirachtin is generally allowed in organic gardening.

 **Sloper Says**

Whenever you bring clones or someone else's starts into your garden assume they have pests and molds. Spray them several times a week for two weeks with Azadirachtin. It's cheap, simple insurance.

Azadirachtin works with multiple modes of action against pests, including repelling them, interrupting their feeding behavior, regulating their growth and smothering funguses. Like sulfur, only use Azadirachtin on cannabis only when flowers are not present. It will leave an unpleasant taste.

Potassium Bicarbonate

Potassium bicarbonate ($KHCO_3$) is used as a fungicide and generally allowable in organic cultivation. It works by altering the pH of the leaf making it uninhabitable for fungi. It's safe for humans—in fact it is used as a food additive particularly as a leavening agent in baking. It only kills what it comes in contact with and does not become systemic within the plant. Multiple applications are usually required. In most circumstances' potassium bicarbonate can be used up to the day of harvest.

Spraying with the Lights On

MYTH Should you spray with the lights on or off? A common misconception is that spraying must be done with the lights off because the droplets form "micro magnifying glasses" that intensify the light at a particular point and burn the plant. Most of the current sprays are fine to spray on cannabis plants with the lights on. The only exception I have found is when spraying heavy horticultural oils.

Anyone who's attempted to burn paper with a magnifying glass knows that the glass needs to be significantly above the paper in order to focus enough light energy on a single point to get it to burn. Simply laying the glass on the paper won't do it. That is a long way of saying spraying with the lights on is fine. If it wasn't, how could plants survive a thunderstorm followed by sunshine?

This myth probably got started after someone used poor-quality or contaminated water when spraying and it damaged the plants. It's more likely that a high concentration of salts in the spray caused the dark-spot damage than the light and droplets. Yet this myth persists. Even if you feel uncomfortable spraying with the lights on in an HID garden rest assured you can safely spray with the lights on in an LED garden.

Too Much Air Movement

Getting air movement within a grow facility is critical. But too much is just as problematic as to little. Far too often I see gardeners, especially at large facilities, blasting the plants with circulating fans. They usually tell me that they are having a problem with powdery mildew (PM) and that's why they need more air flow.

Unfortunately the extreme air flow can be contributing to the PM issue. When a plant is strongly blown by the wind it closes its stomata to keep from drying out. This can back up water stores in the plant. When the wind stops, the plant releases this water– sometimes quickly. This can add to local high humidity and leave water on the plant–the very things all that blown air is trying to relieve in the first place.

 **EXPERT CORNER**

Powdery mildew grows best in high humidity but sets off its fruiting bodies (the white stuff in technical terms!) in low humidity. If you're trying to fight PM don't drop the humidity too low as an attempt at a cure. Treat, and move the air gently.

Cleanliness is Next to Godliness

We have all heard the phrase "cleanliness is next to godliness" and it's never more true than in a grow facility. Indoor gardening is inherently a dirty practice, especially when growing in soilless mixes.

During the Grow

Keeping your garden clean during the grow is very important. Clean everything you can, anytime anything looks like it needs cleaning or picking up. Dead leaves provide a haven for pests to hide and multiply. They can also spawn fungus and mold and clog drains, causing flooding. If anything is spilled, clean it up right away. When the floor of your grow space is clean, you can notice problems such as nutrient leaks before they become major events.

Post-Grow Clean-up Procedures

After you have completed your grow, it's time to clean up. There is no right or wrong way to do this as long as you get the grow space completely clean. This is a critical step that is often skipped or skimped on in order to get the next crop going faster.

Assuming you didn't have pest problems, all you need to do is thoroughly wash everything used in the garden. Use a 1:10 dilute bleach solution to clean all racks, trays, buckets, reservoirs, pumps, hoses, timers, controllers, and pruners as well as the floor, walls, and ceiling. Wipe off all of the equipment in the grow space including fans, filters, dehumidifiers, ladders, stools, and lifts. Make sure to rinse everything that comes inContact with the plants several times with plain water to completely rinse off the bleach. Another great alternative to bleach is hydrogen peroxide–but be sure to dilute the solution as well and wear gloves to protect your skin!

If you did have pest problems during your last grow, you'll need a more aggressive cleanup. Start by removing all traces of plants from the garden. The type of infestation will dictate the cleaning needed: if you had fungal attacks, bleach the entire room—walls, floor, ceiling, doors, and fixtures—with full-strength bleach.

 **Good Practice**

After a harvest is a great time to check all the fuses in the garden. Many timers and controllers use fuses. A corroded fuse has been the cause of many garden failures.

Make sure you have adequate air flow while cleaning, or wear a respirator, as bleach fumes are not good for you. Wear rubber gloves, long sleeves, and long pants to protect your skin. If you had pest invaders such as spider mites make sure everything is dead—including the buggers hiding in the cracks. No matter what method you choose, make sure everything is dead, gone, and cleaned up before starting another crop in that space.

Commercial growers might have other options. Currently there are businesses being established to clean your grow facility at the end of each grow cycle. They know what chemicals/treatments are allowable in your local area and have better equipment. Commercial grows can also include UV light and ozone in post-grow cleaning protocols, as previously discussed, as long as appropriate safety precautions are taken.

Clean the Lights

Probably the most important part of the post grow cleanup to cleaning the lights. Most growers spray their gardens as part of their integrated pest management program. No matter how careful you are, some spray will always get on the lights.

This is a problem as dirty optics can cut the transmission of light by 10% or more. Make sure to thoroughly clean the lights after each grow cycle. Being able to clean them is the reason why having strongly protected emitters is a requirement for a commercial grade LED grow light.

Greenhouse growers should deploy lights with a minimum IP 65 rating so the lights can be cleaned with a pressure washer. This saves a significant amount of time versus wiping each one individually. Indoor growers can get away with IP ratings as low as 55. Thoroughly wipe these lights with a soft lint-free cloth and a dilute hydrogen peroxide solution on all surfaces (lenses, housing, heat sink and cords). Contact the manufacturer of conformal coated LED grow lights for proper cleaning procedures.

12. Final Thoughts

Even with everything we've covered so far, there are still a few thoughts to pass along that just didn't seem to fit anywhere else. With these final thoughts in mind, you'll be ready to tackle your first LED grow, or to start improving your garden if you're already growing with LEDs and want to step up your game.

"LED Grow Lights Don't Work" [...for them]

If you've hung around a hydroponic shop, online indoor garden forum or a gardening tradeshow for any length of time, you've heard this: "LED grow lights don't work". Many self-purported "experts" have had trouble using LEDs and feel the need to tell everyone. It's like they're garden lighting superheroes out to save the growing community from a dire threat. Not even willing to have a conversation, most of these blowhards just bash anyone and everyone who even mentions the three evil words– "LED grow lights".

Don't let somebody else's bad experience limit your options. I've communicated with a lot of these growers, and almost without exception they bought an early or cheap LED grow light (or built their own from cheap components) and/or have limited-to-zero gardening skills. They try to use an LED grow light exactly the same way they would use an HID light, which from reading this book you know is a recipe for disaster. Their stories mostly go the same: he or she tried growing with an LED light, and based on poor results part way through the grow, they switched back to an HID to save their harvest. That's not an experiment. That's just a regrettable grow.

These people will never learn new tricks, because they are unwilling to experiment and *learn* from the results. Change is hard for some people, and that's OK. One size generally does not fit all. LED grow lights are not for everyone.

My advice–just like the old joke of adding "…in bed" when reading a fortune cookie–is to mentally add "…for them" whenever you hear or read someone say that LED grow lights don't work. Simply walk away from these people and think to yourself, "LED grow lights don't work… for them". We all have different goals in our lives as well as our gardens. Blanket statements like "LED grow lights don't work" are just plain silly and expose that person's inability to adapt.

Not Trying to Reproduce Sunlight

One of the things I can't stress enough is that we're trying to grow plants indoors, not reproduce sunlight. Many times grow lights are compared to the sun, with some light manufacturers bragging about how much better their light is because it more accurately reproduces sunlight. After all, the sun is the "big bulb in the sky" under which everything grows, so this makes a good sales pitch.

Don't get caught up in the hype. As we discussed in the photosynthesis and photomorphogenesis section the thing your garden wants when it comes to light is sufficient quantities of the right spectra to fuel photosynthesis and photomorphogenesis. Keep your eye on the ball. Mimicking the sun is not important. Strongly driving photosynthesis and photomorphogenesis are, and that is what LED grow lights are designed to do.

Be a Gardener, Not an Engineer

Keep focused: the point of gardening is to produce big, good-tasting harvests, not to build the most elaborate grow room. Too much of the time, growers focus on their grow room, attempting to precisely control each variable (temp, humidity, CO_2, etc.) until the garden itself becomes an afterthought. These "engineer growers" are not done until there is at least one of every gadget in the grow room. They want to check all of their meters and controllers before making a decision. Don't be this type of gardener.

True gardeners check their plants regularly and respond to what the plants are telling them. They know what to look for, and if they see a problem, they have an idea about the possible culprit even before glancing at their meters and gauges. It's better for your garden and your wallet for you to develop these skills before you run out and buy more gadgets. You'll probably kill a few plants in the process, but you will learn. Unfortunately, there is no substitute for experience. Be this type of gardener.

Experiment to Completion

Experiments have little value unless taken to a true end point that has meaning. For example, when experimenting with different cloning techniques, you need to take some using your regular method and some with the experimental procedure. Both sets need to be grown to maturity and then the results compared. You can't base your "results" on how fast the cuttings root or how bushy the roots are, or you might be missing something important.

These clones need to be grown and harvested to really know if there's a difference. You might be creating a "robbing Peter to pay Paul" situation: something you did to decrease rooting time might cost you later in harvest size or quality. Interim results are helpful for understanding how your change affects the process, but the only result that truly matters is your harvest.

After you've completed your experiment, do it again several times to see whether the result was real or a fluke. When you can consistently produce the same results from the same experiment after multiple tries, your results begin to have merit. Then try it *this* way, and *that* way, and *the other way* too–repeatedly, until you've exhausted every way you can think of and have a large collection of results. Only *then* will you have a dataset from which you can begin to draw conclusions. Experimenting is not a one-time thing. It's a process that takes method, time, repetition, consistency, and patience.

On the subject of experimenting, to know anything for sure, you need these experiments to be based in real science–your eyes or taste buds won't replace scientific instrumentation. Multiple "runs" on a chemical analysis machine such as a gas chromatograph–mass spec machine (GC-MS) or atomic absorption instrument are necessary to provide real answers. In order to gather any real information, multiple samples from varying heights, nodes, or branches, not just the top pinnacle fruit, from multiple harvests must be averaged to produce real data.

Quantifying a Harvest

Grams per Watt

Every gardener likes to brag about harvest size. The most common way indoor gardeners brag is to quote their yields in terms of weight per watt of electricity consumed. For example, if a grower produced 1,000 grams under a 1000 watt HID lamp, the harvest would be described as "one gram per watt".

This is a terrible way to measure garden output. The first problem is that a 1000 watt lamp can consume up to 1,100 watts depending on the ballast, so the "watts" side of the equation is likely off. Secondly, electricity used to power the ventilation systems, air conditioning, nutrient pumps, timers, and controllers doesn't get added into the watt count, so the "watts" are even farther off. These extra watts can really change the "grams per watt" calculation. Unless the entire grow room is on a separate electric meter, it's almost impossible to determine the actual electrical consumption. Anything else is an estimate.

It's OK to use grams per lamp size to tell if your harvest weight went up or down for any given harvest, but it's no good for bragging rights. Besides, grams per watt focuses on the wrong thing–the weight instead of the quality of your harvest. Let the other growers brag all they want–just show them your harvest. If you've done a good job, your harvest will speak for itself.

Gram per Watt Days

A more valid way to quantify the harvest weight is to include the concept of time–grams per watt days. If you grow 100 pounds in 100 days and someone else grows the same 100 pounds but in 80 days who's got better results? Just mentioning how much was grown per amount of electricity without adding in a time factor really means nothing yet people brag about it all the time.

To make this problem worse–you also need to include the electricity used while the plants were in the vegetative state. What if one gardener veg'd his plants for 50 days and the next is veg'ing for 30 days, who is getting better results? Neglecting to report this electrical consumption continues to cloud the situation.

Ease per Weight

It's far more valuable, in my opinion, to focus on "ease per weight". Considering ease per weight helps you focus on making changes that make gardening easier on *you*–things you can do, buy, or change to spend less time and effort while maintaining a healthy and bountiful indoor garden. This is one of the driving forces that led me to experiment with LED grow lights: I needed a garden that produced less heat and consumed less electricity, because I spent way too much time stressing about summertime high garden temperatures and inflated utility bills.

Along the way I made other changes, such as switching from hydroponic methods to charged soilless mixes so I could primarily feed with water–eliminating clogged feed lines, simplifying spill cleanup, and getting rid of the stinky slime in my reservoir that required odor control during a grow and aggressive reservoir scrubbing after harvest. These changes dramatically simplified my gardening life and over time improved the quality and quantity of my harvests.

Quality per Harvest/Gardening Zen

Which leads us to the most important garden performance metric: "quality per harvest". Who cares if you can grow tons of inedible junk? Indoor gardening is about growing *the largest quantity of the best quality you can for the least expenditure of resources*. After all, you're spending your life energy in your garden. You should reap the benefits of that effort by producing the best that can be grown. Quality per harvest is where bragging rights are properly placed.

Increasing harvest quality while maintaining weight, minimizing watts used, and simplifying the experience should be every indoor gardener's goal. There are thousands and thousands of ways to grow plants indoors. Rarely, if ever, is a particular technique or product critical to the success of a garden. The gardener's skill, and a little luck sometimes, matters much more.

Thus, even though LED grow lights forever changed my gardening life for the better, they might not work for you. It's OK if they don't–though if you follow the advice in this book, they probably will. Constantly scan the horizon for new products or techniques that address the challenges you're experiencing in your garden. *Thoughtfully try new things, find what works for you, make it easy, and make it your own.*

This is gardening Zen. Namaste

About the Author

Christopher Sloper began his gardening career at 10 years old when he moved into a new house that had a suitable space for an outdoor garden. Although barely strong enough to use a shovel, he worked the soil until plants would grow. Sloper's indoor gardening career began during his undergraduate studies. With a lack of gardening space, but desire for his own *home-grown*, he turned to hydroponics.

Ultimately this led to Sloper's ownership of two hydroponic shops, an indoor growing consulting practice, and his current position as Chief Horticulture Officer at FOHSE, through which he has designed and/or operated dozens of grow facilities with a focus on automation and harvest consistency. His main goal is to properly educate growers and cut through the crap often found within the indoor gardening community.

With a bachelor's degree in Chemistry and an MBA, Sloper is one of the few who is not only an outstanding grower, but can also develop a brand, sell the harvest and most importantly, know how much profit was generated.

Made in the USA
Lexington, KY
24 November 2019